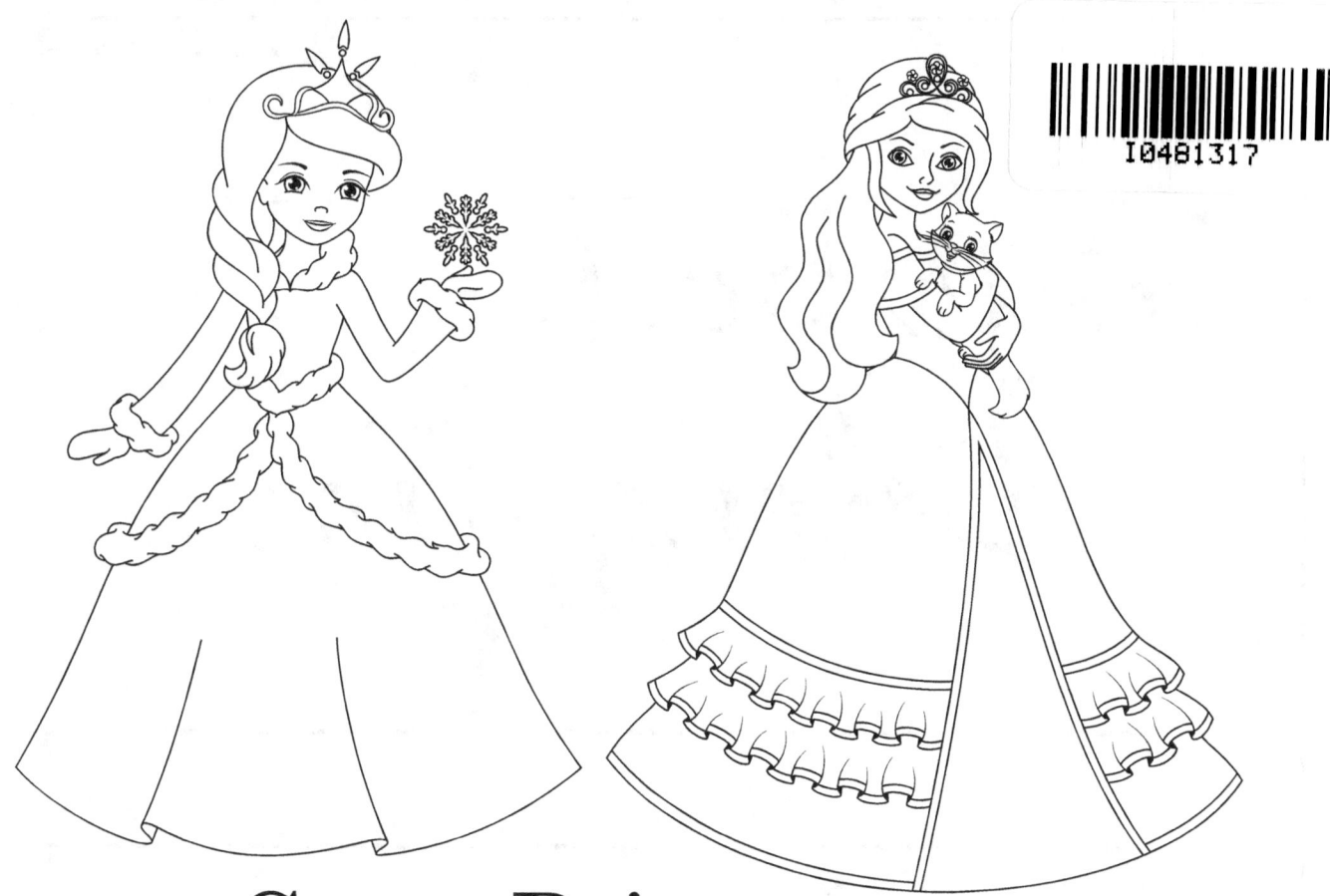

Cute Princess
Coloring book for Girls

Copyright © 2018 Adriana P. Jenova

First edition: First printing
Illustrations and design © 2018 Adriana P. Jenova

Author Contact
Facebook page : www.facebook.com/Adrianapjenovacoloringbook

A finished coloring page, why not frame it? It's a good thanks to brag a brilliantly colored piece!
If you're using a skinny board, it will then be placed into a frame.
Or select a thick board which will be displayed on its own.

This Book Belong To:

_____

_____

_____

_____

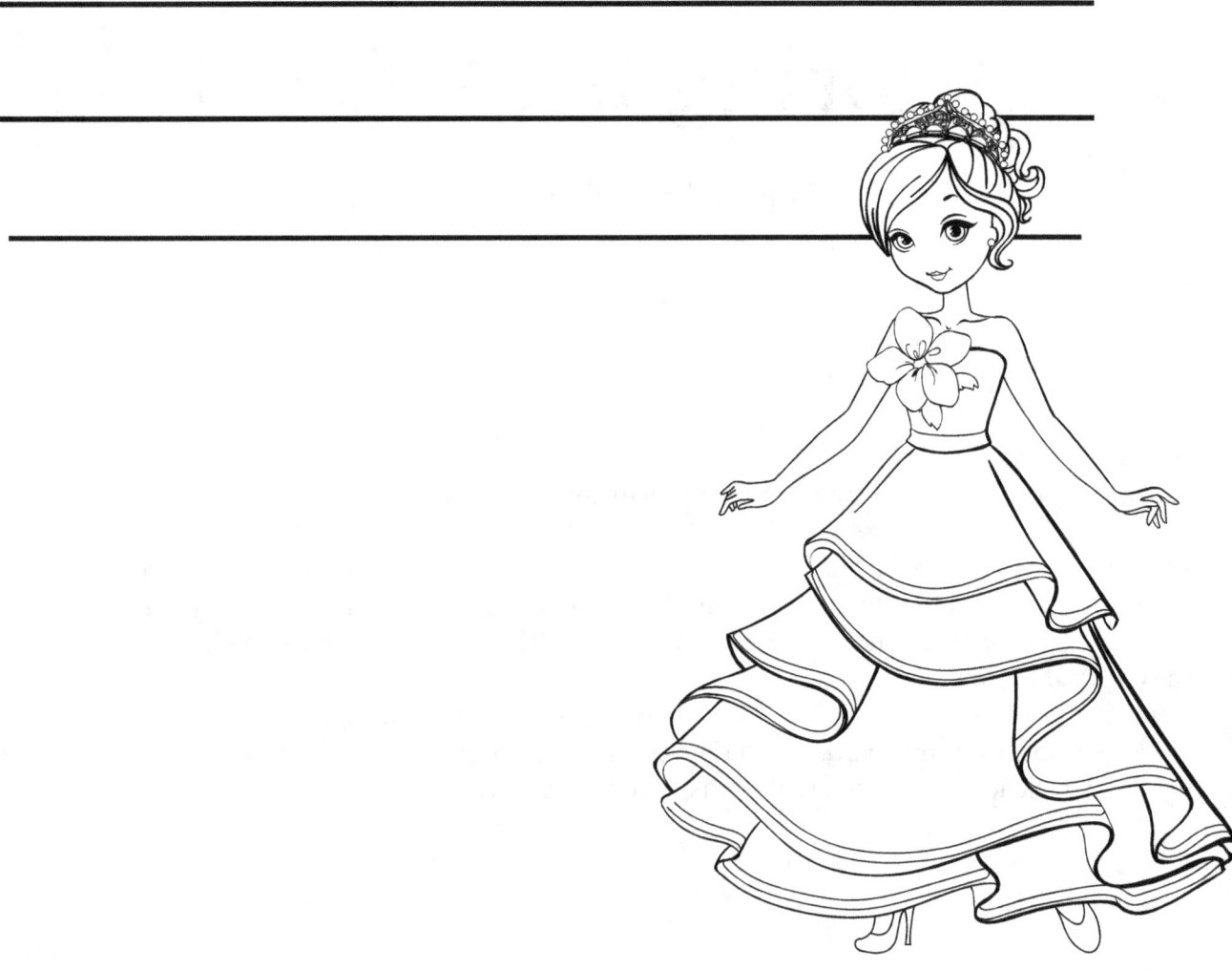

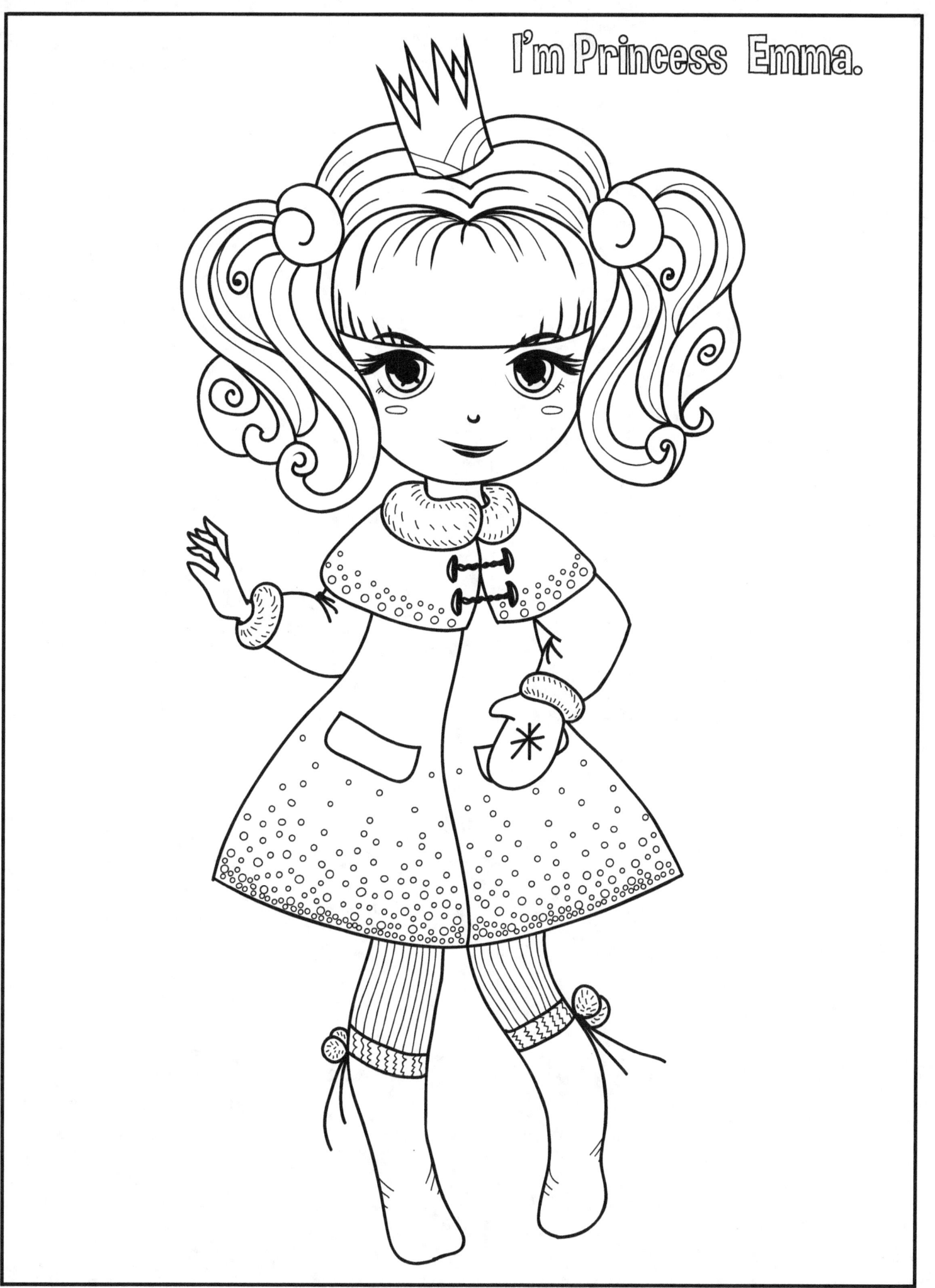

I'm Princess Emma.

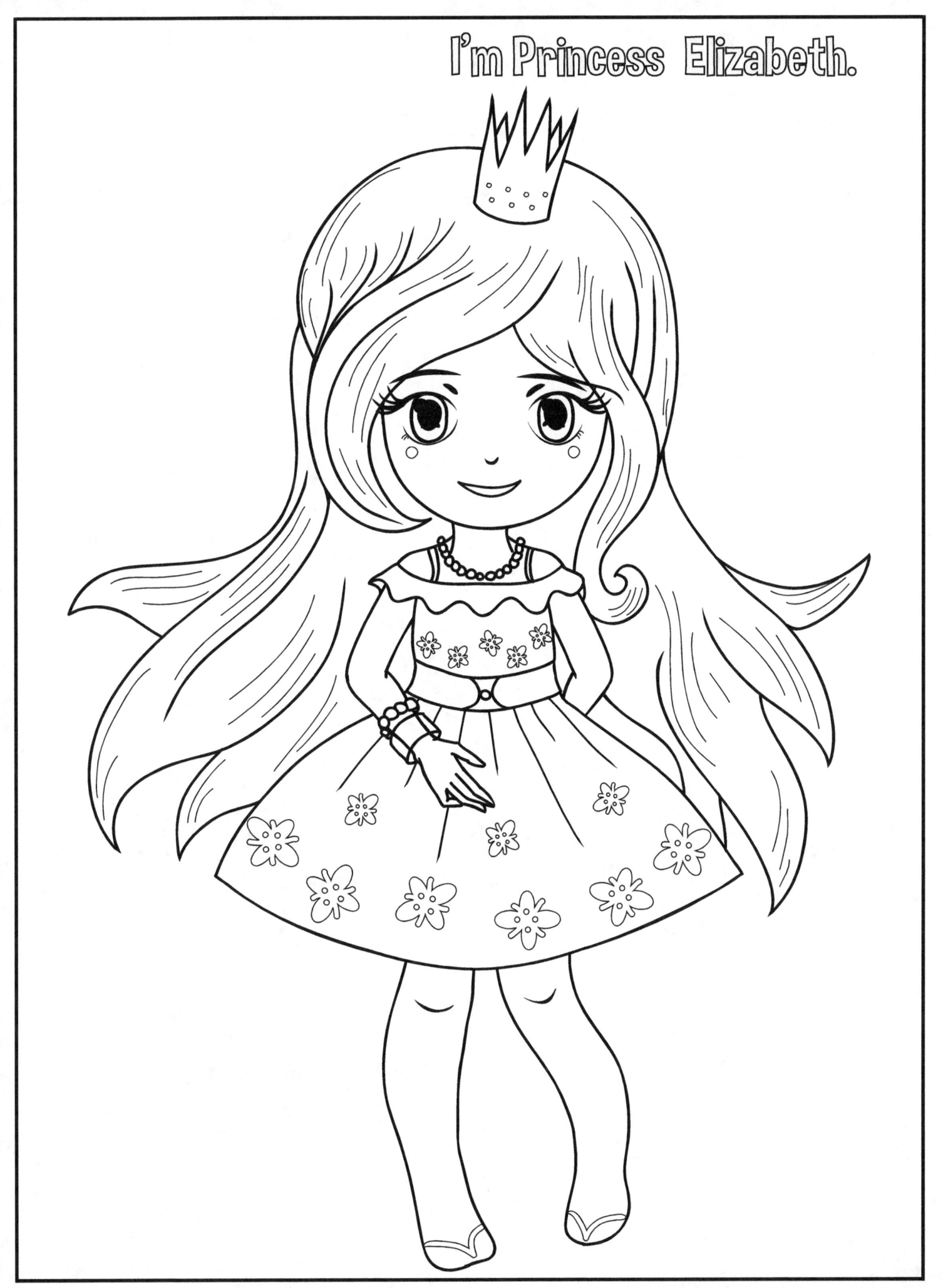

I'm Princess Elizabeth.

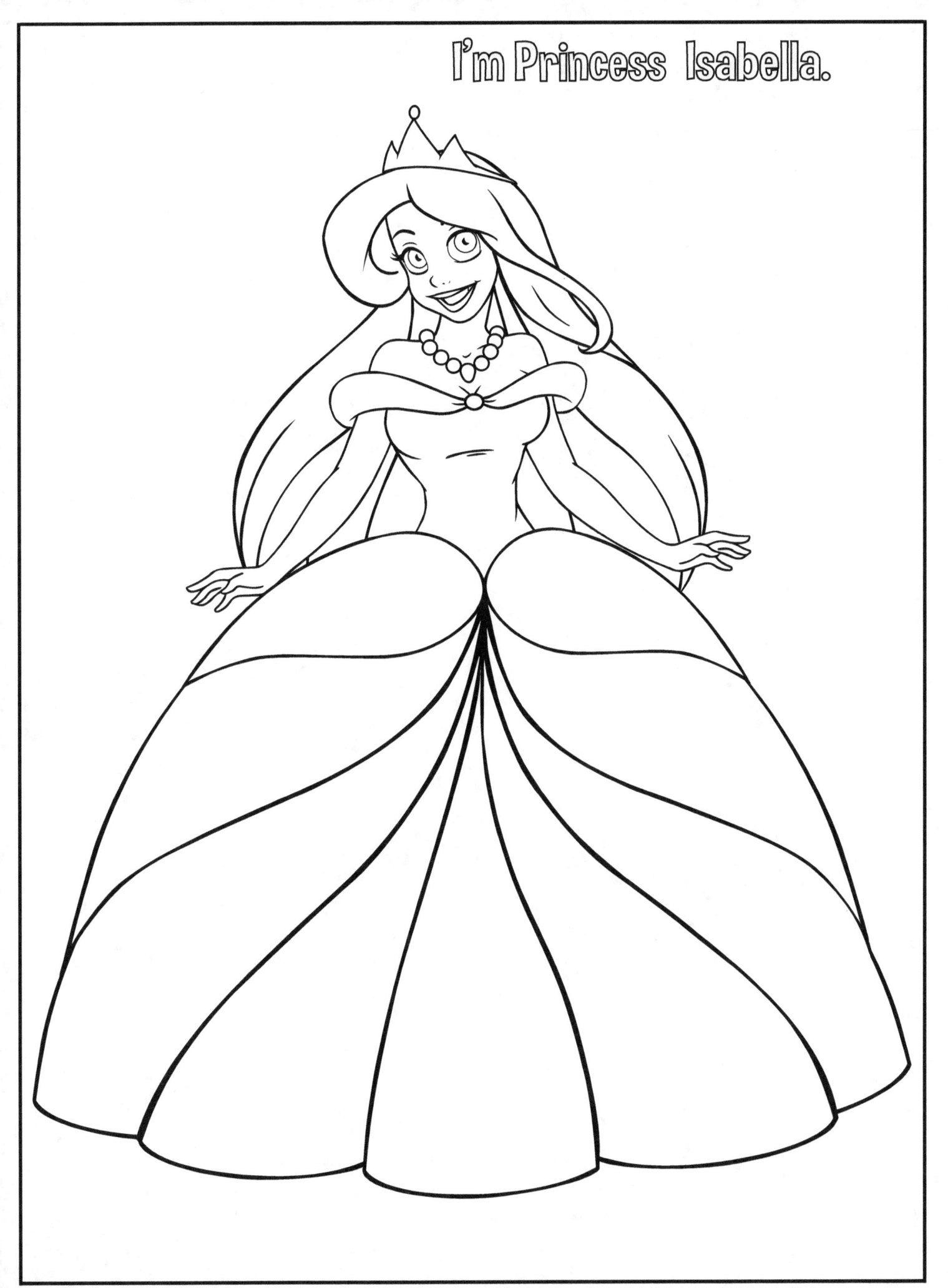

I'm Princess Isabella.

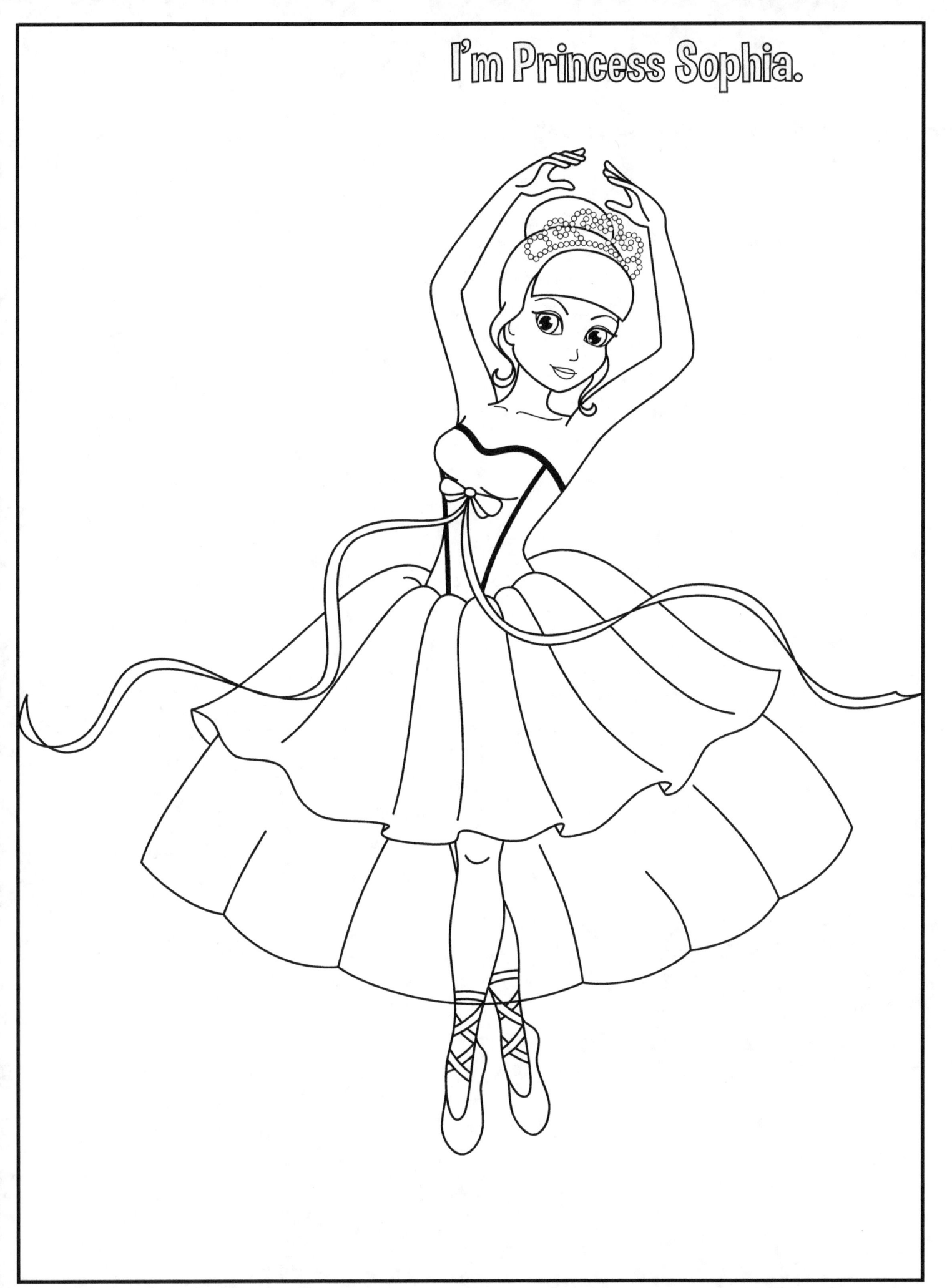

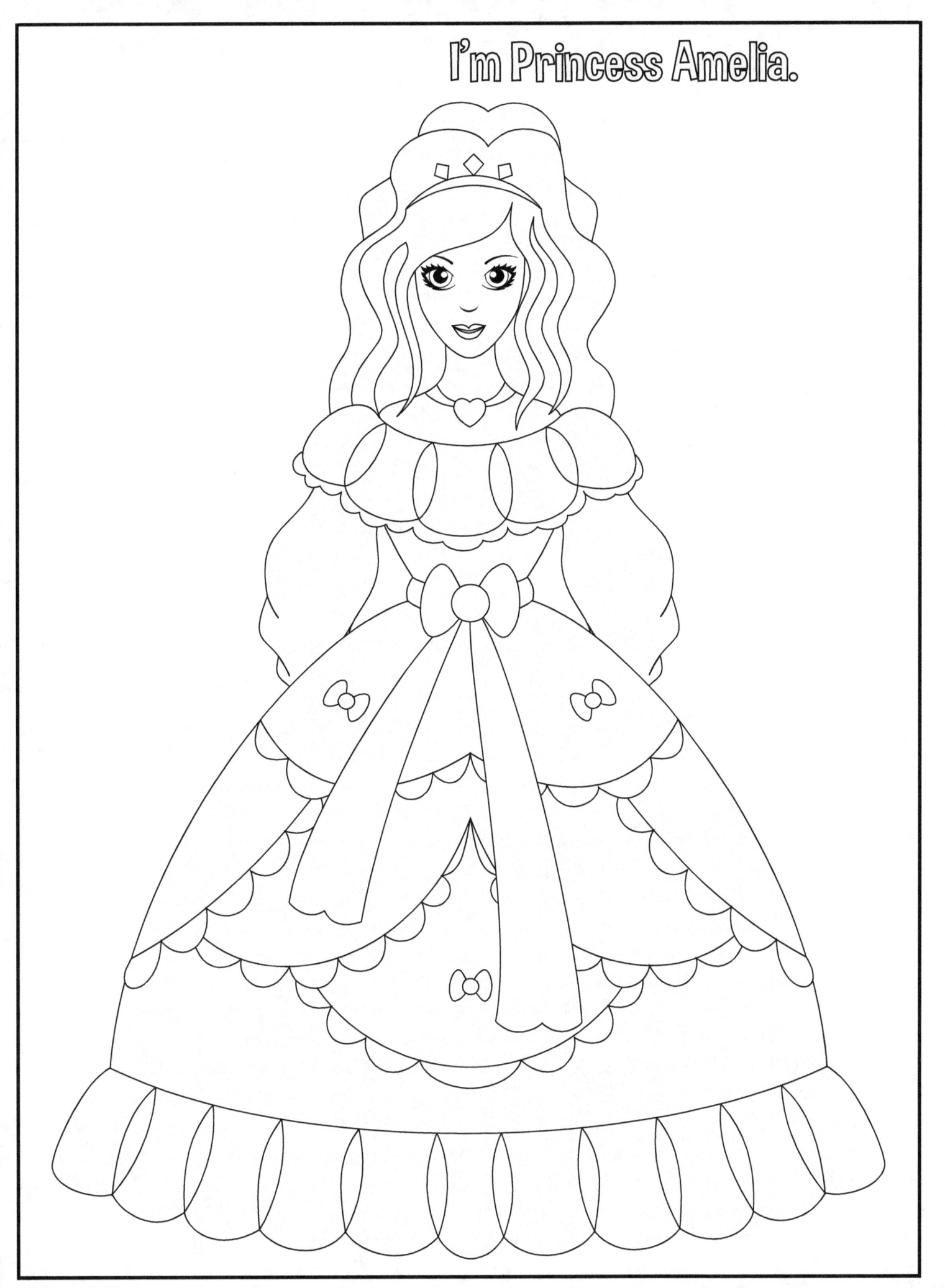

I'm Princess Amelia.

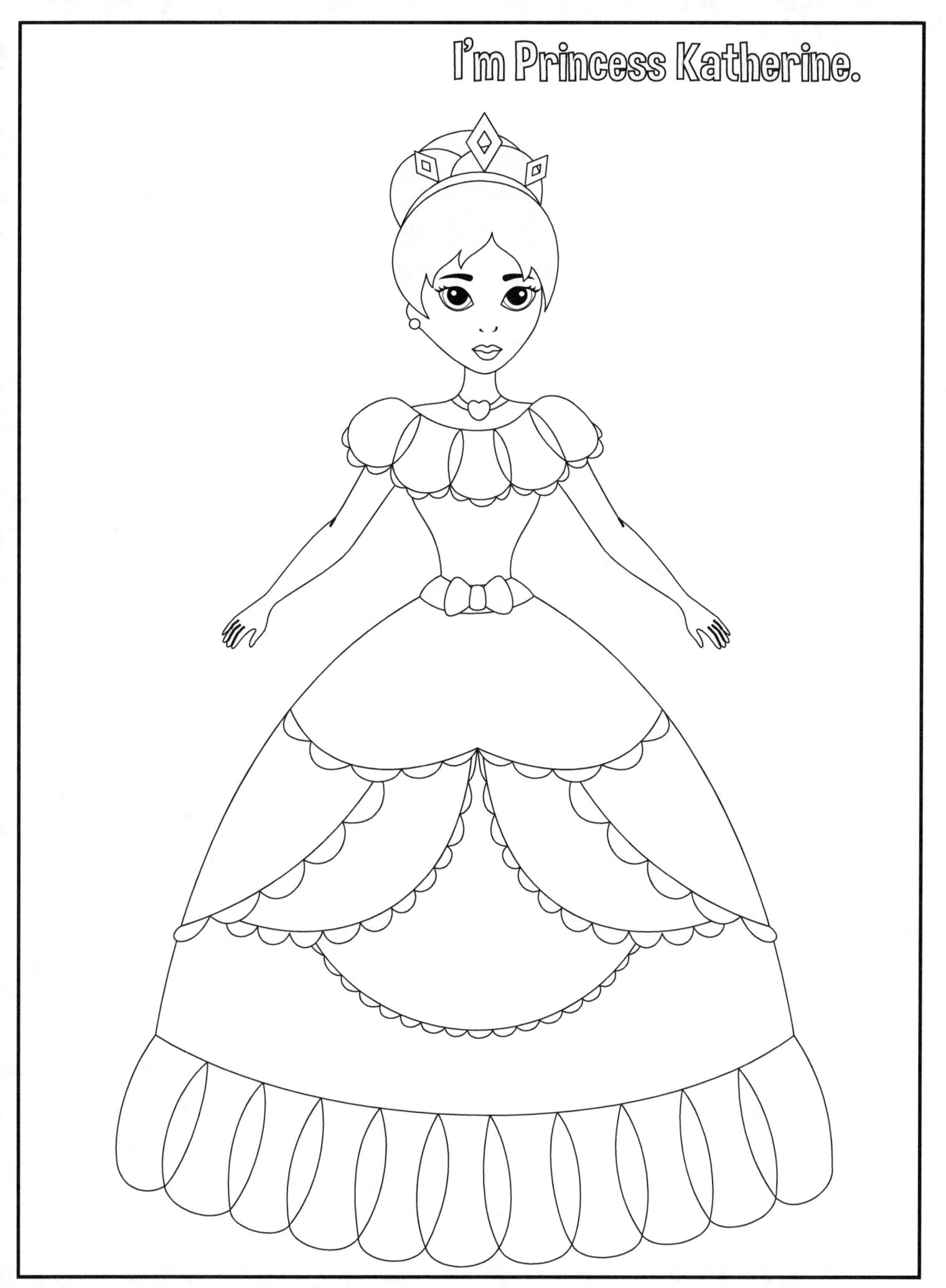

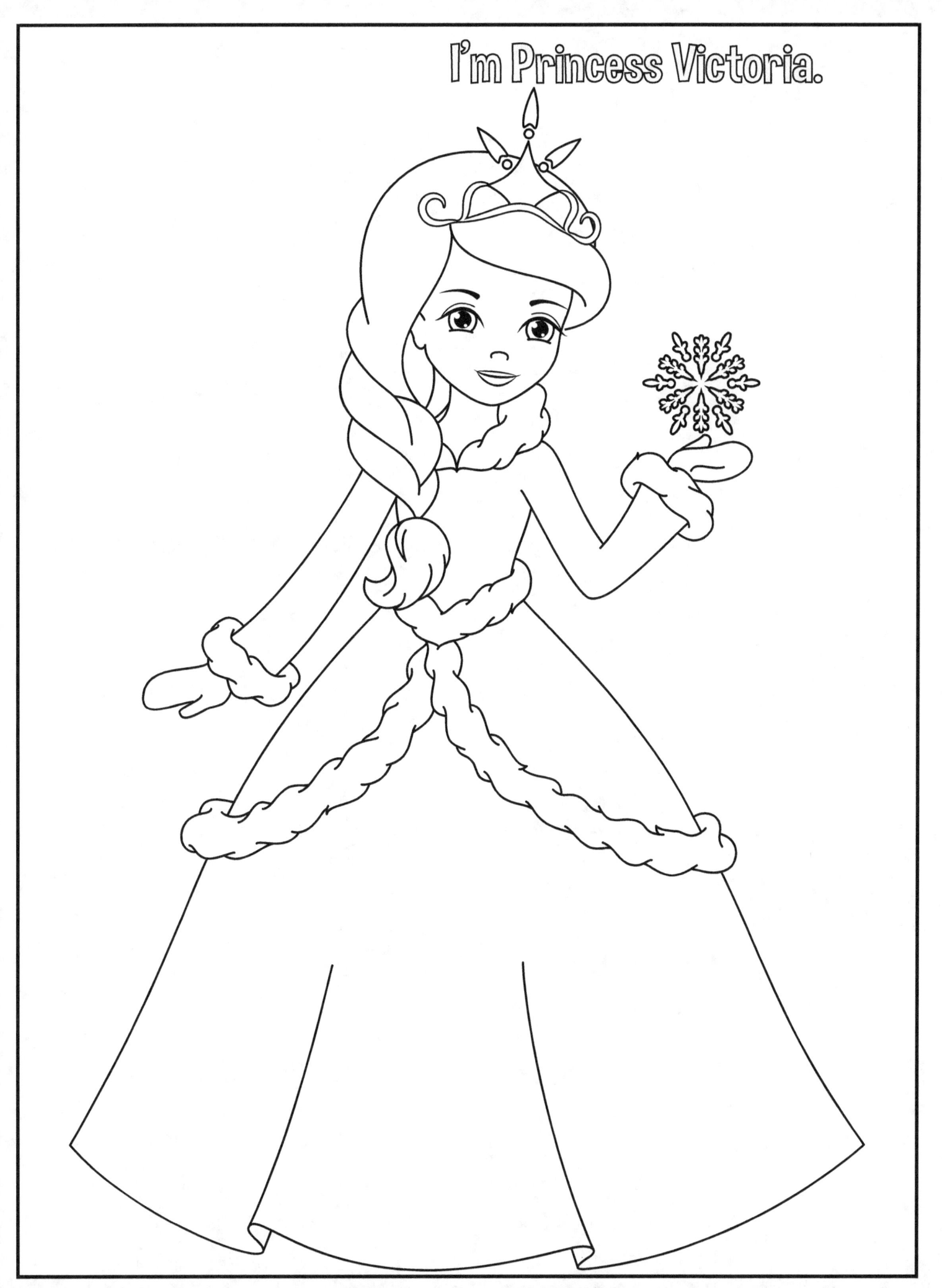

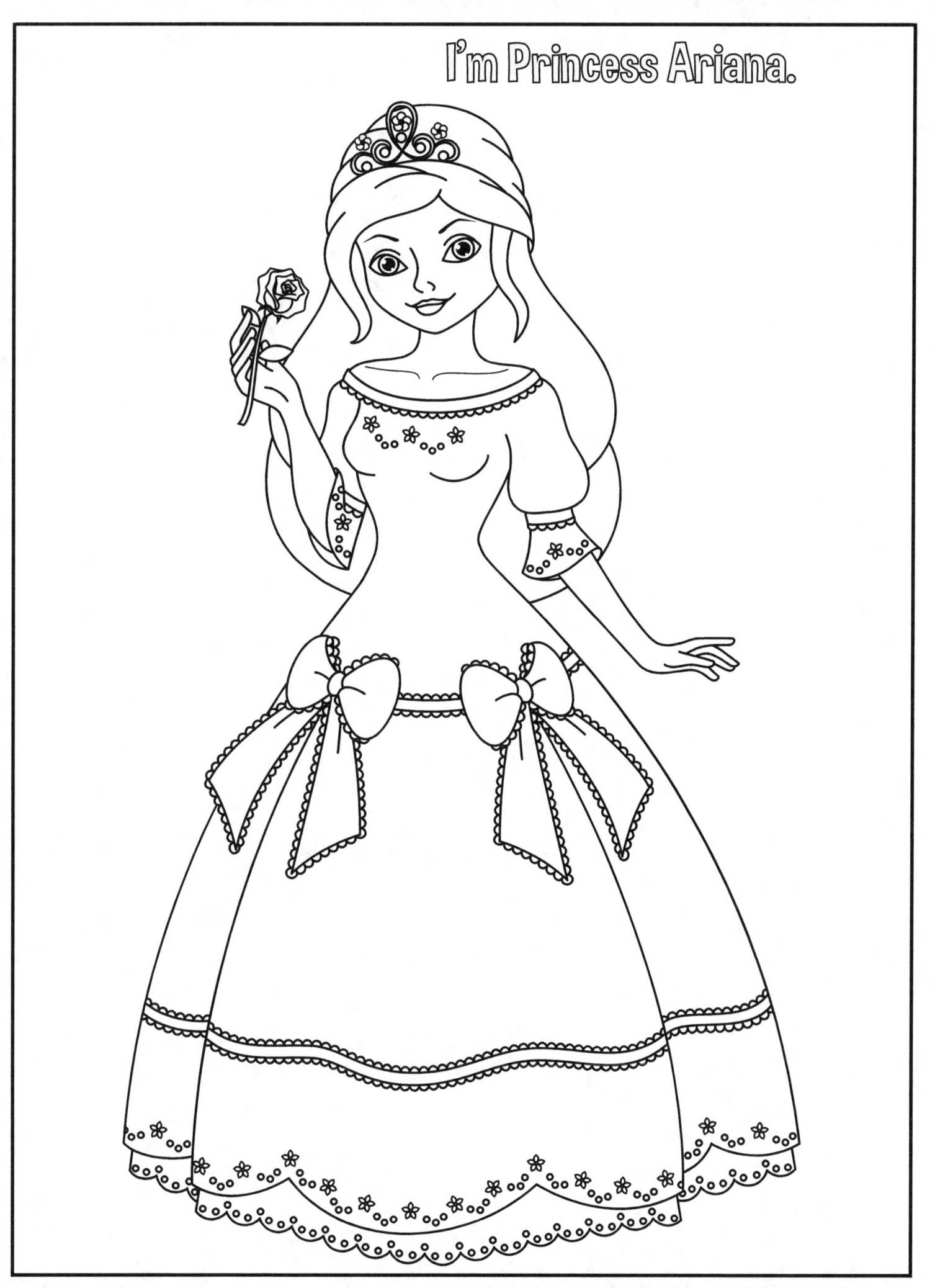

I'm Princess Ariana.

I'm Princess Jasmine.

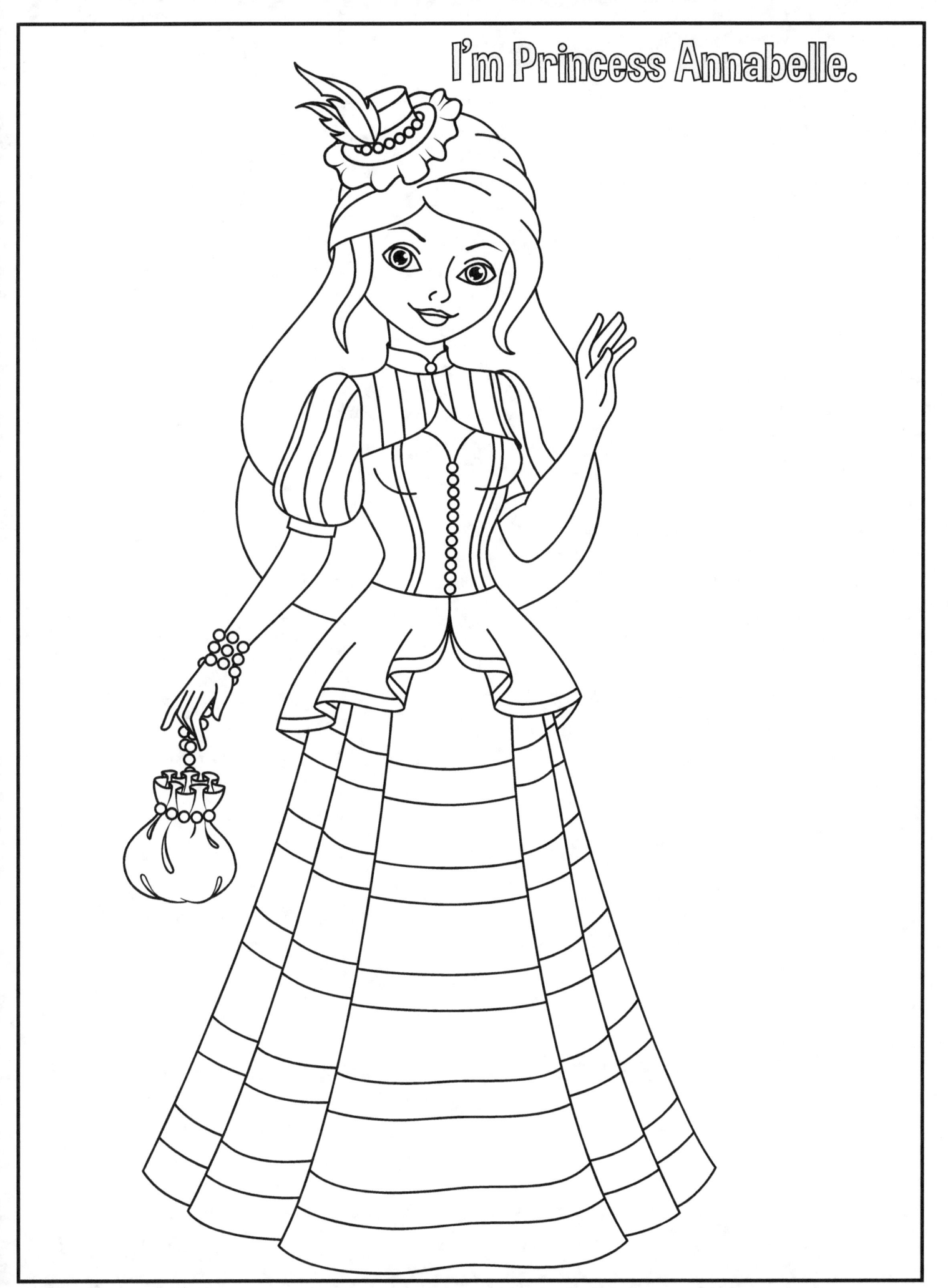
I'm Princess Annabelle.

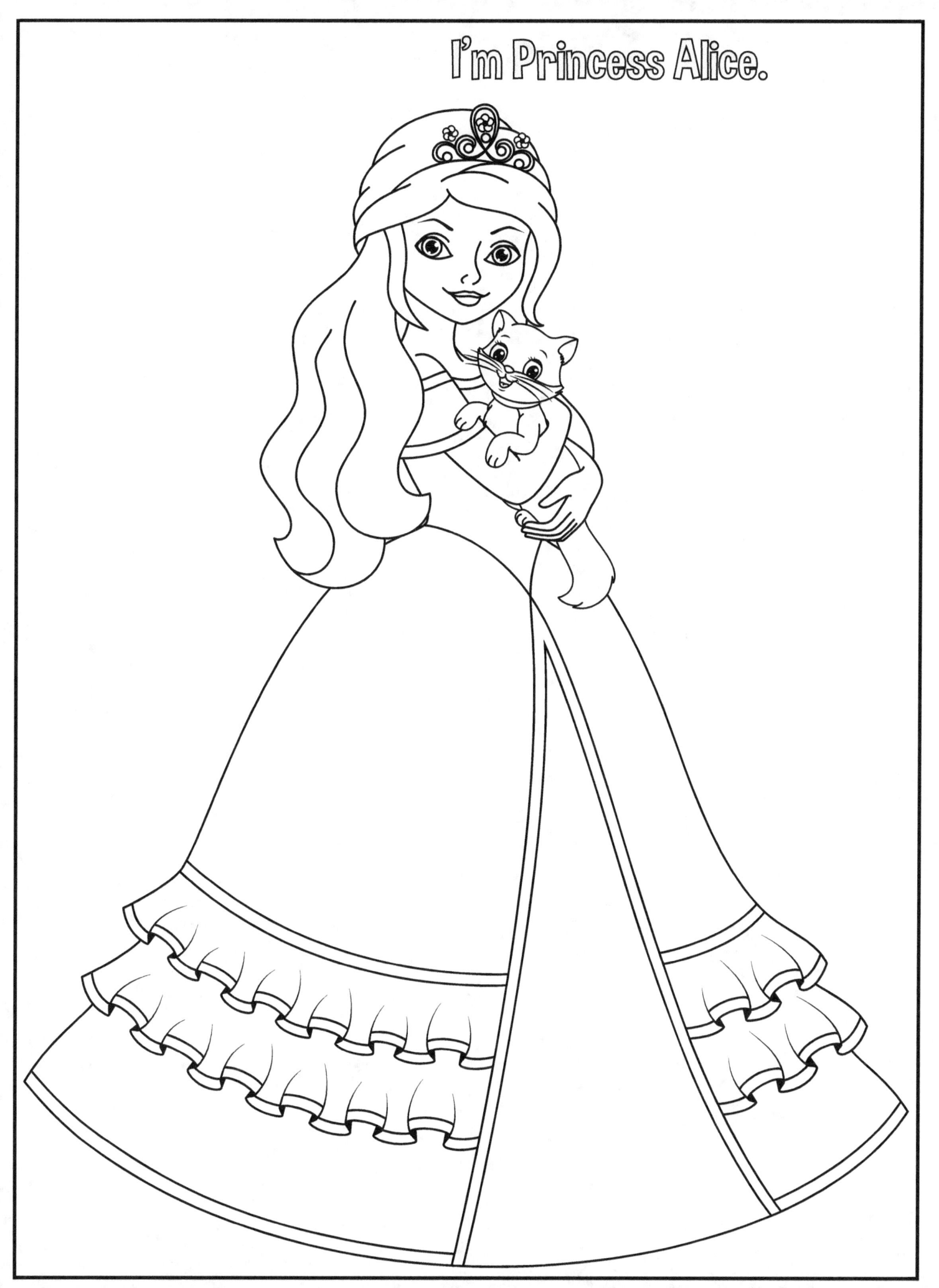

I'm Princess Alice.

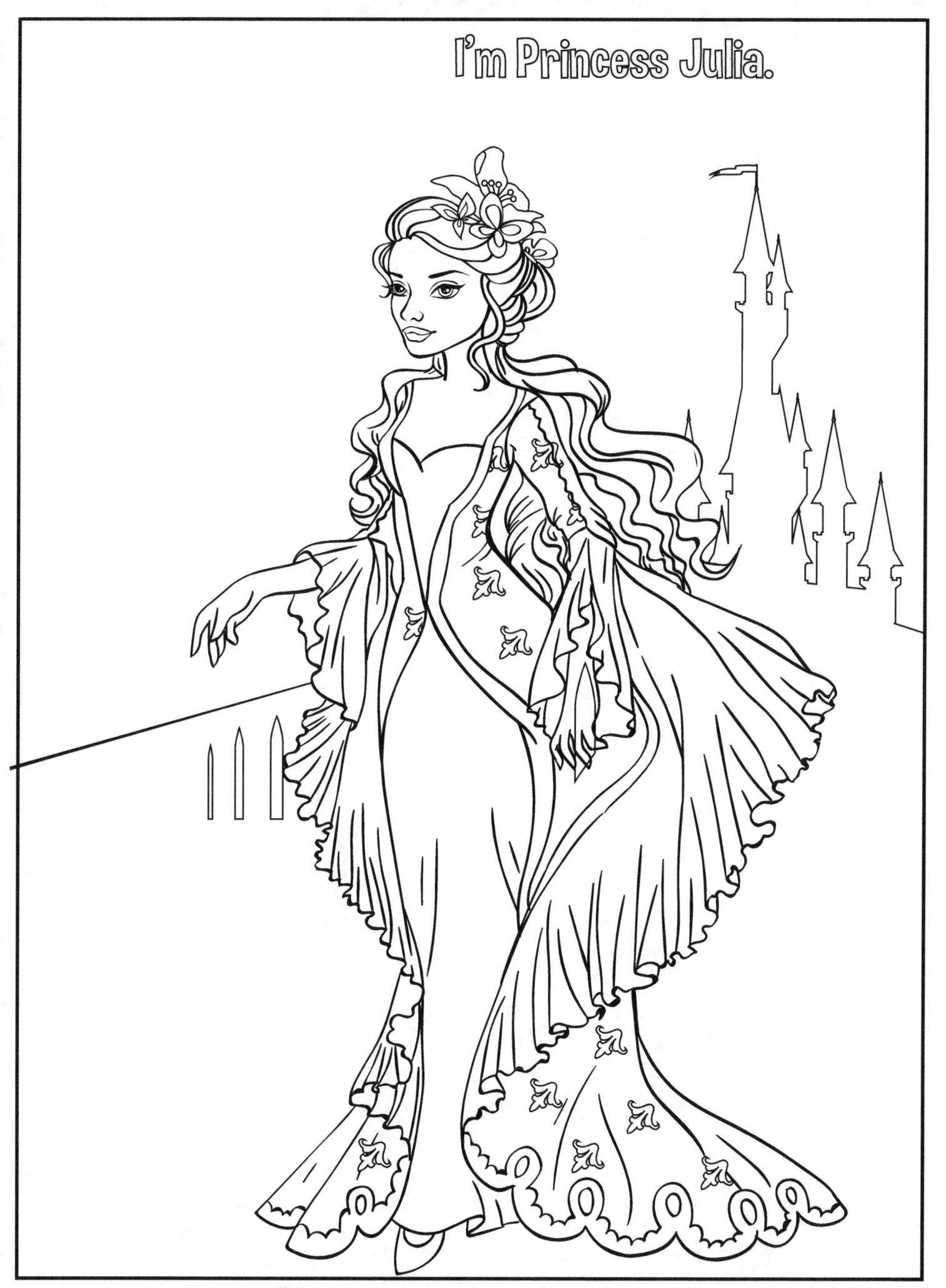

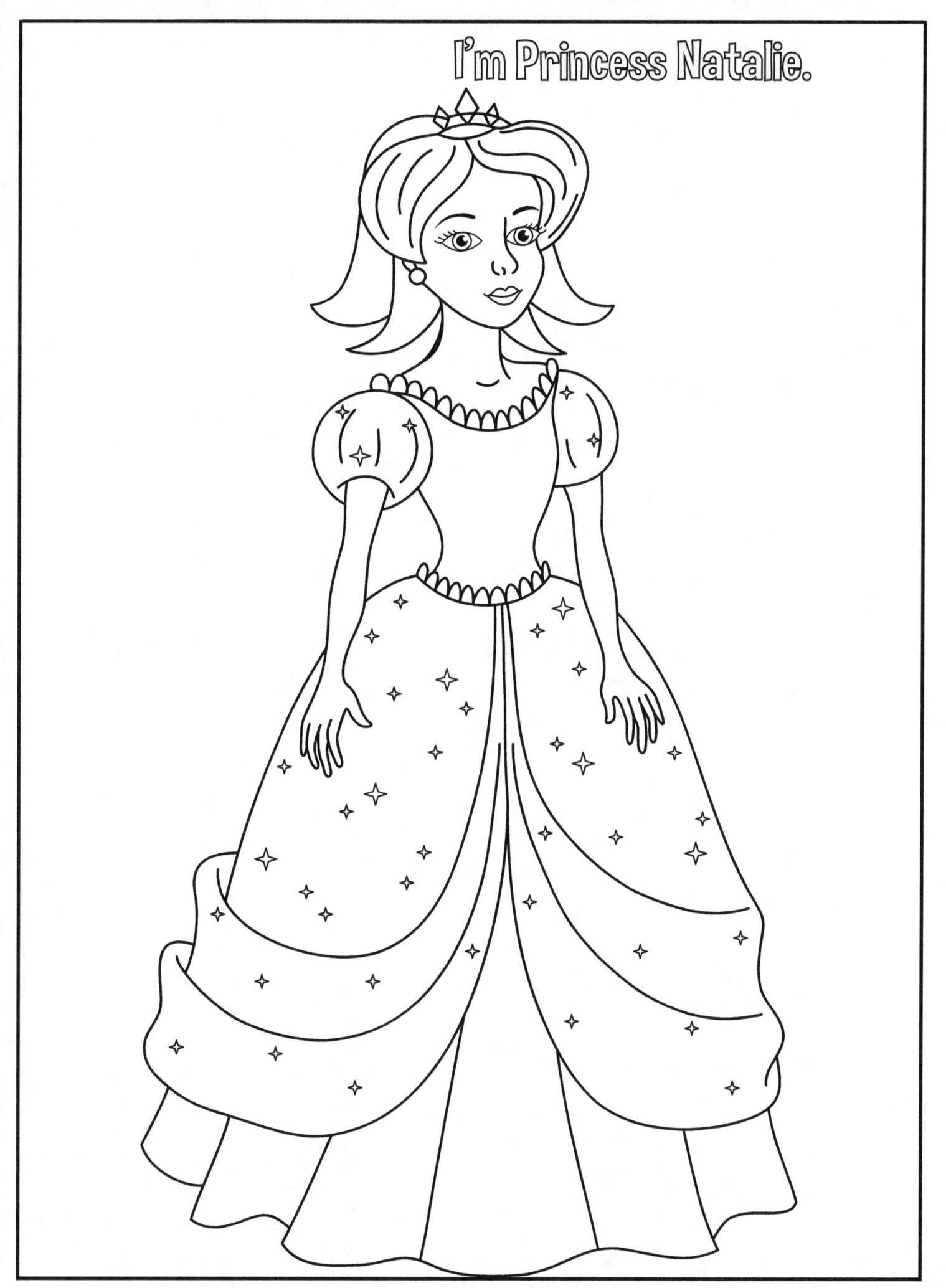

I'm Princess Natalie.

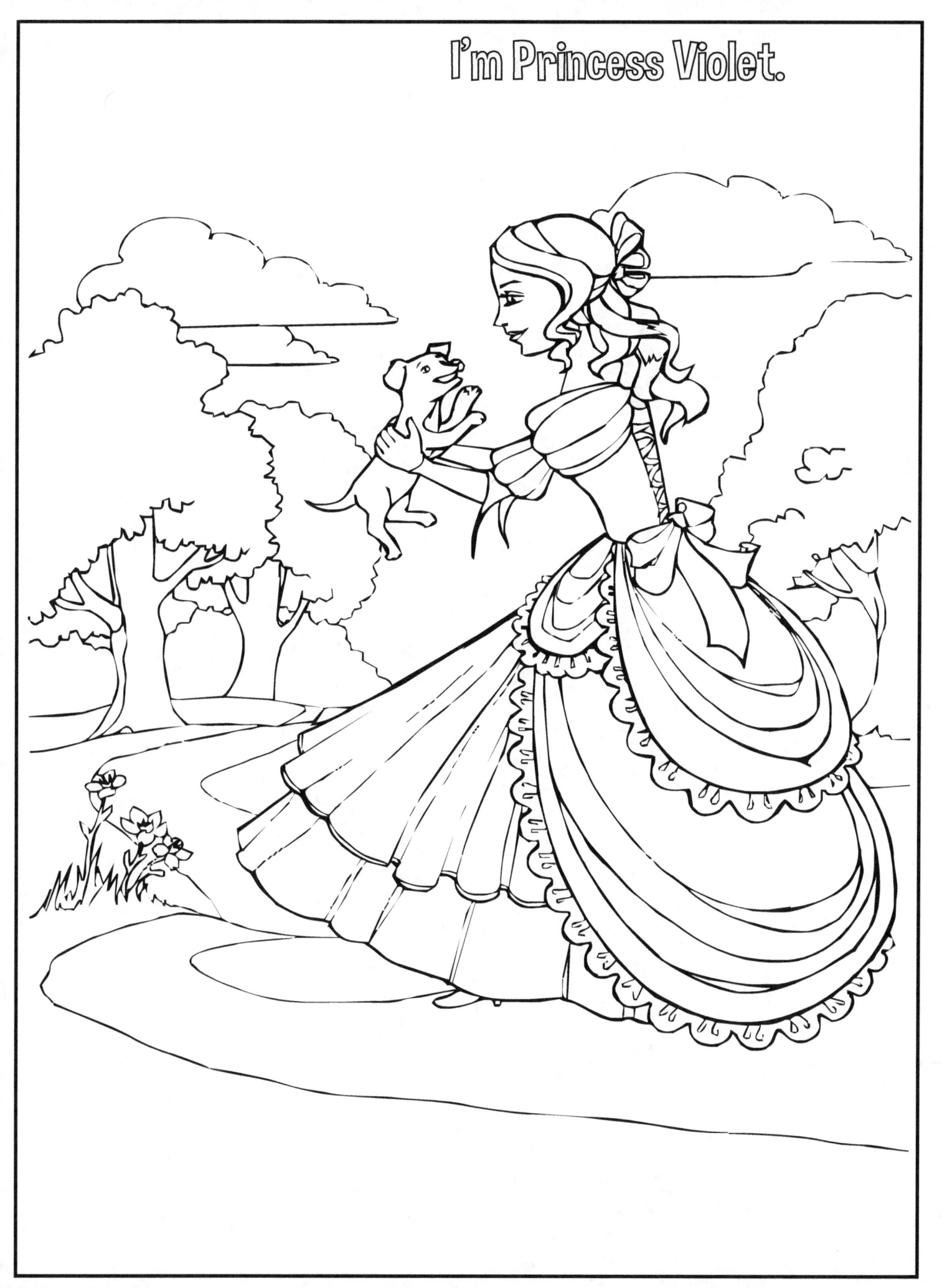

I'm Princess Violet.

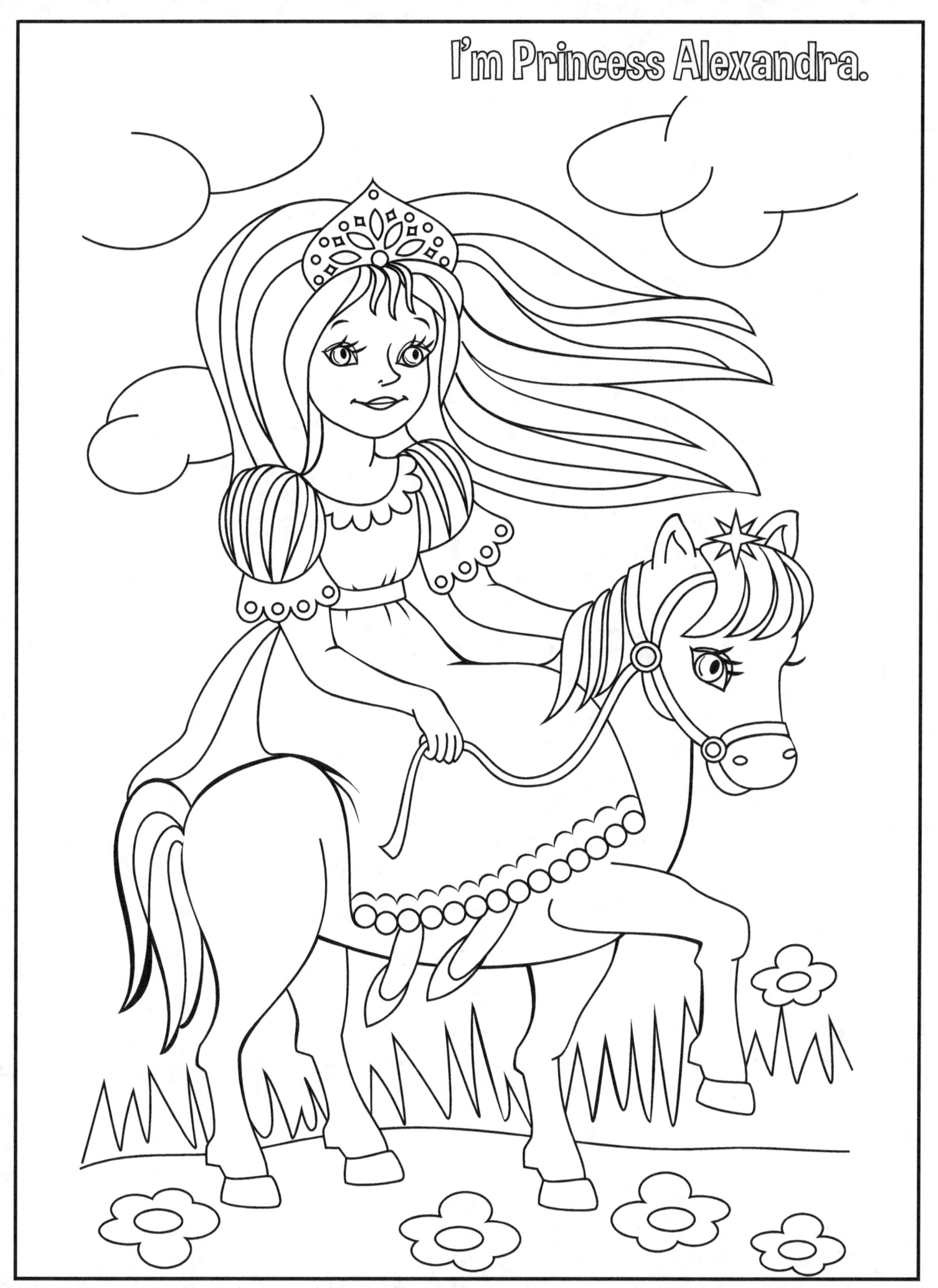

I'm Princess Athena.

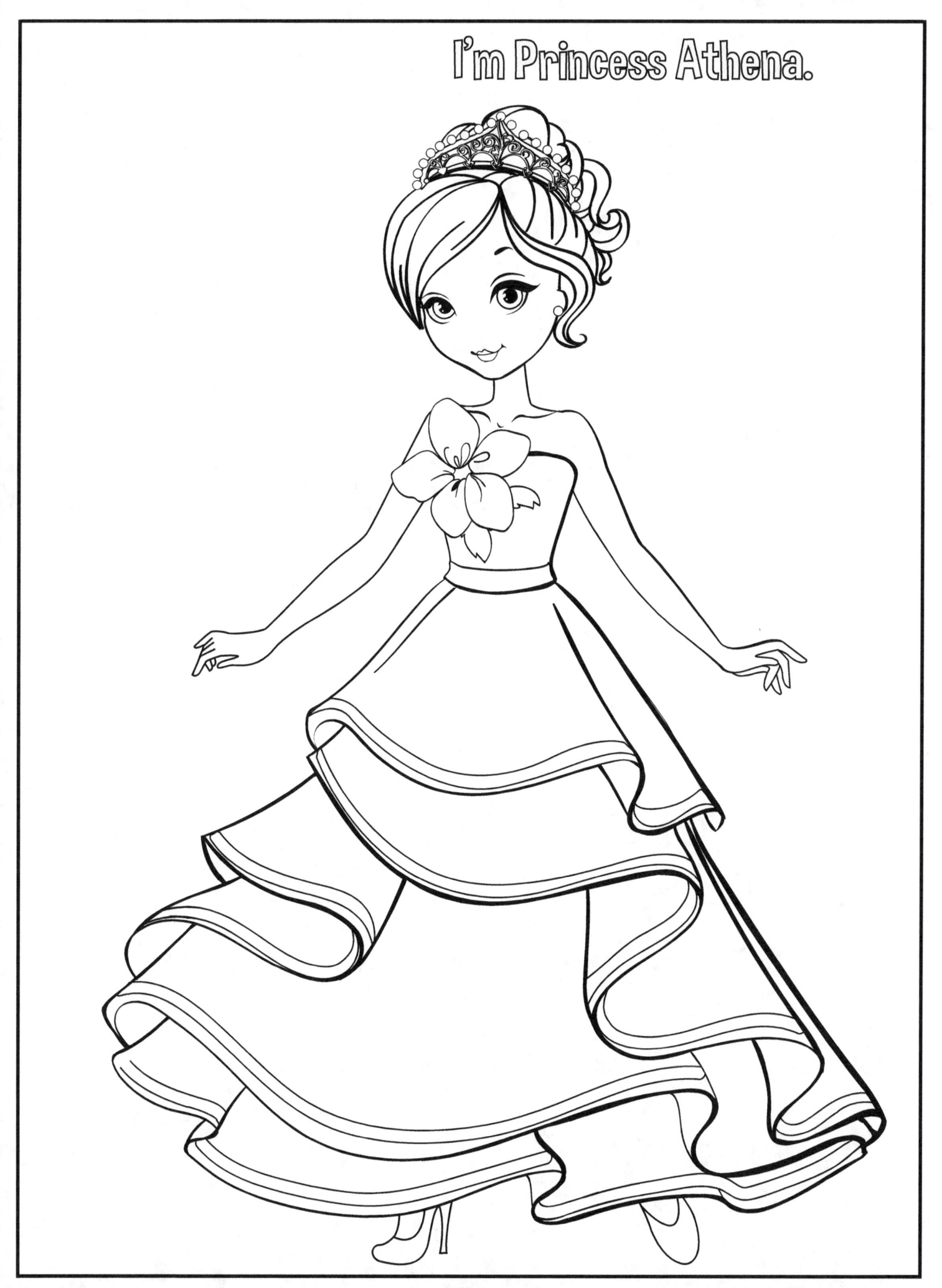

I'm Princess Lilly.

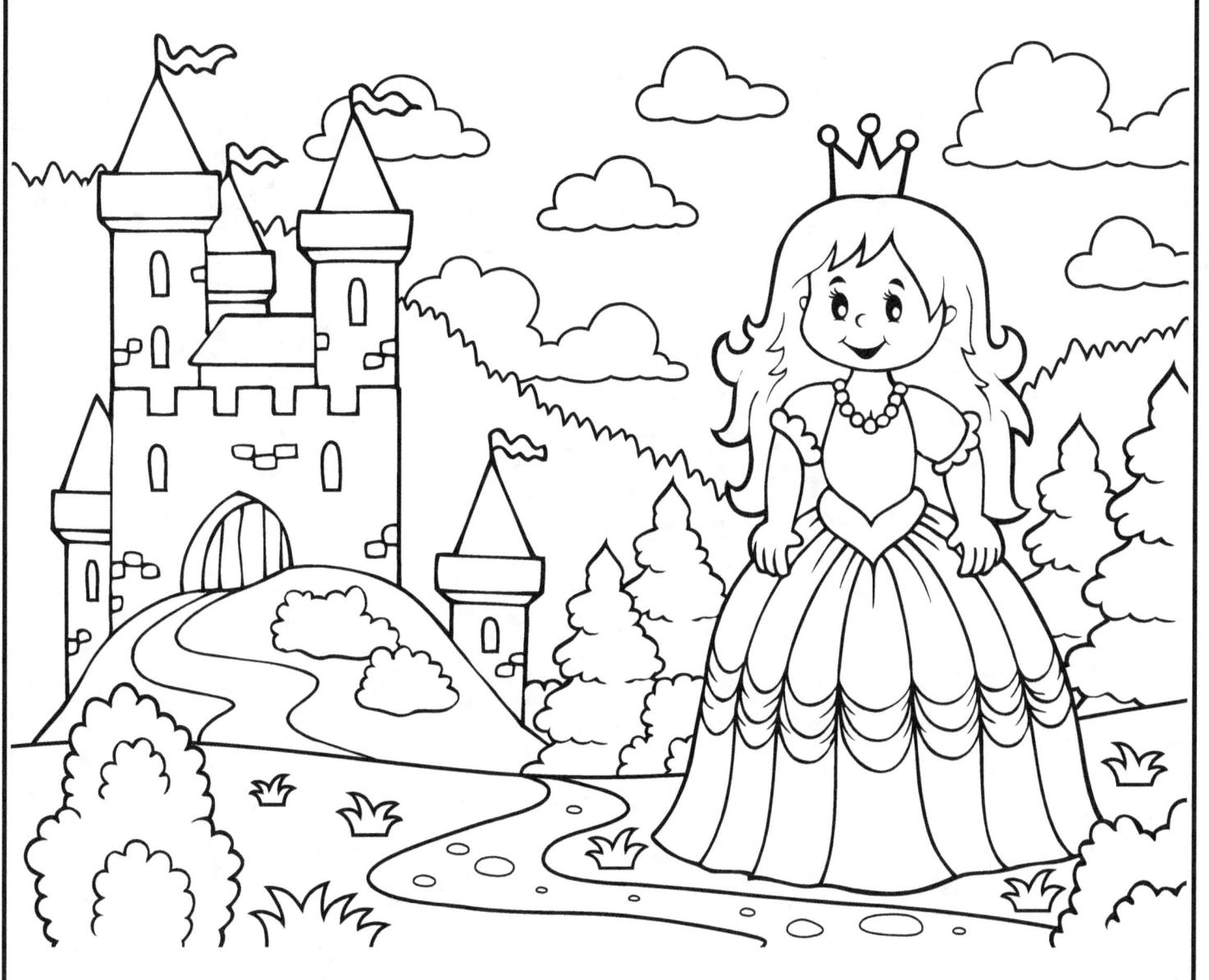

I'm Princess Kimberly.

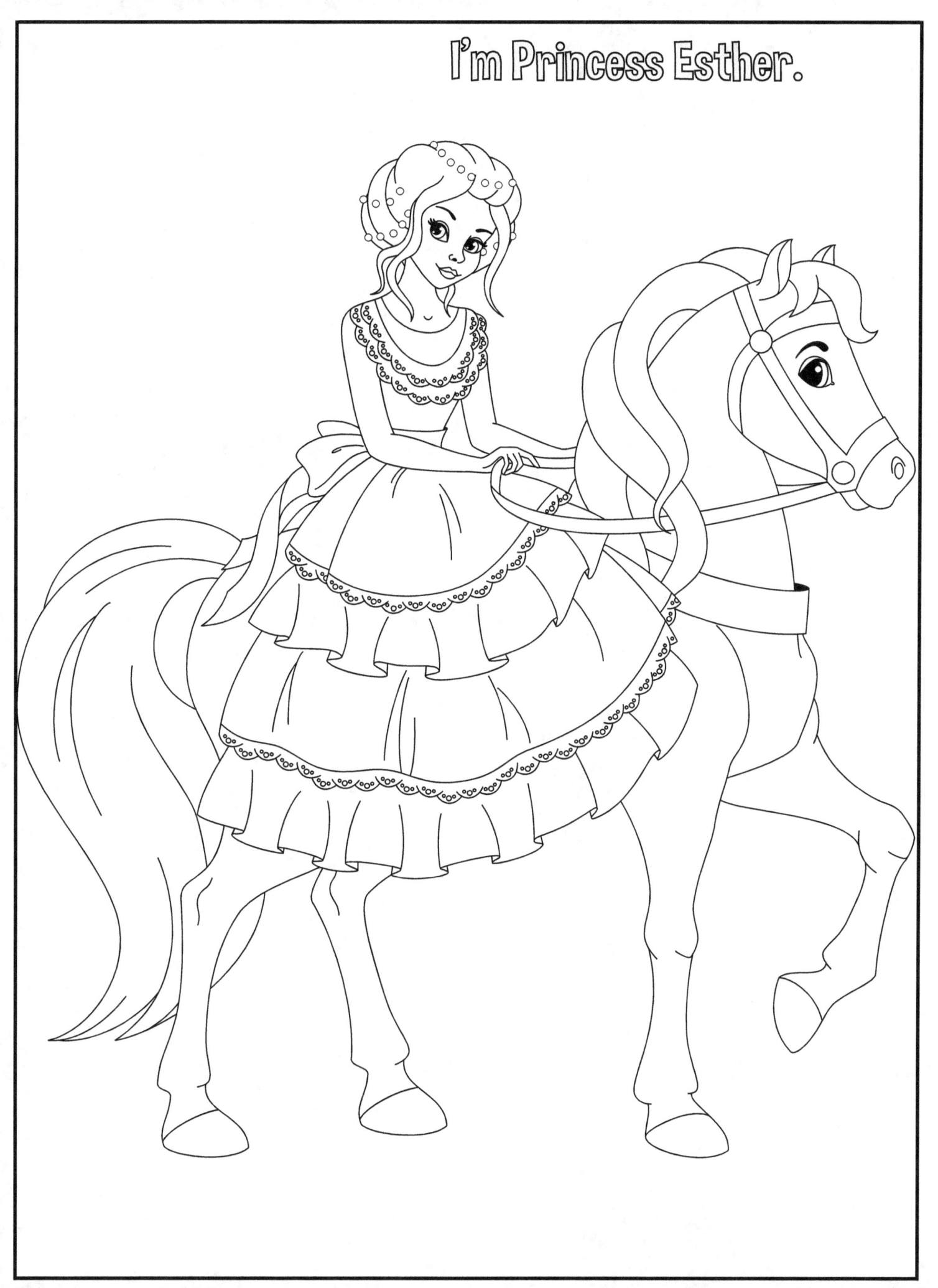

I'm Princess Esther.

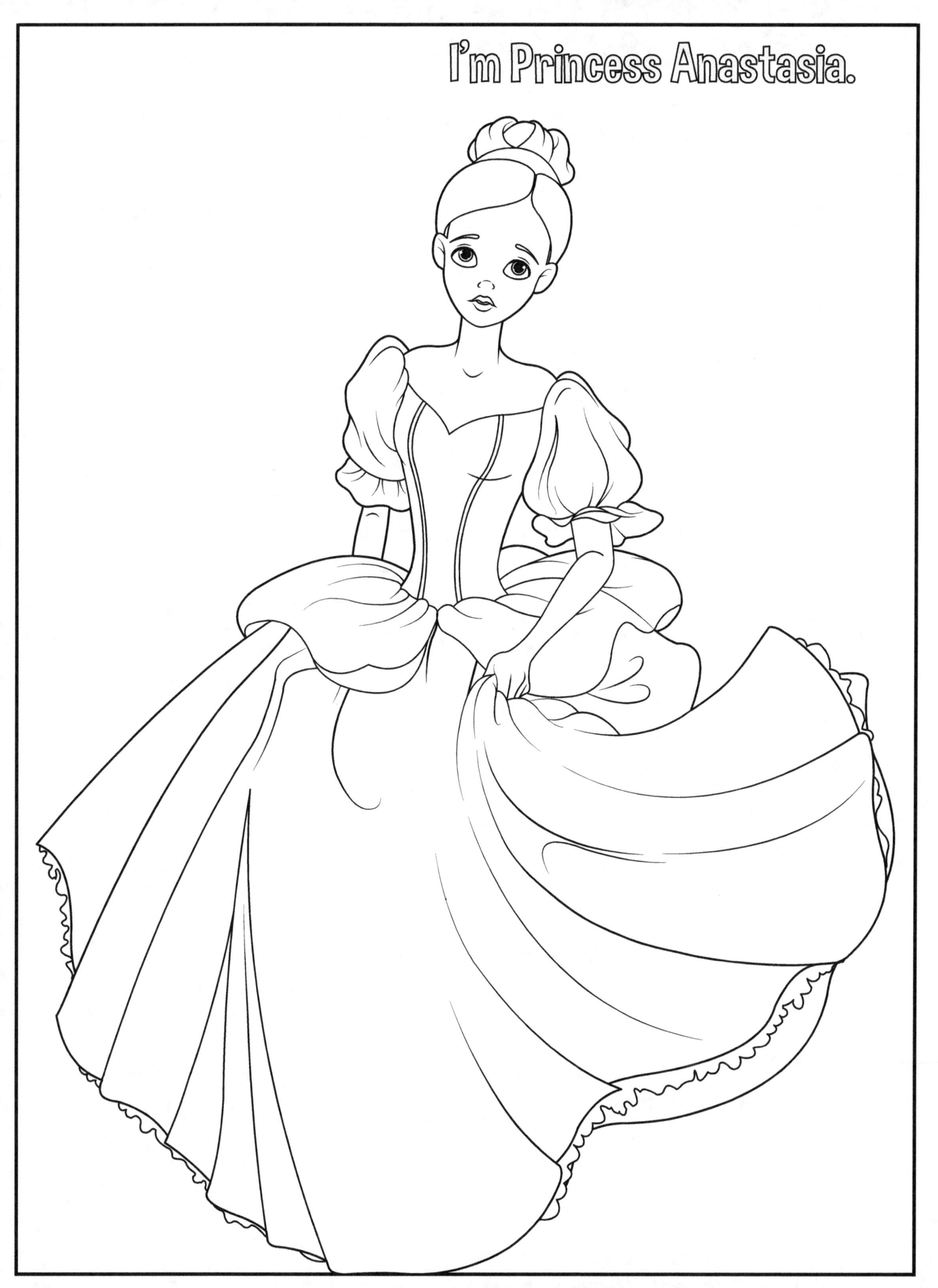

I'm Princess Anastasia.

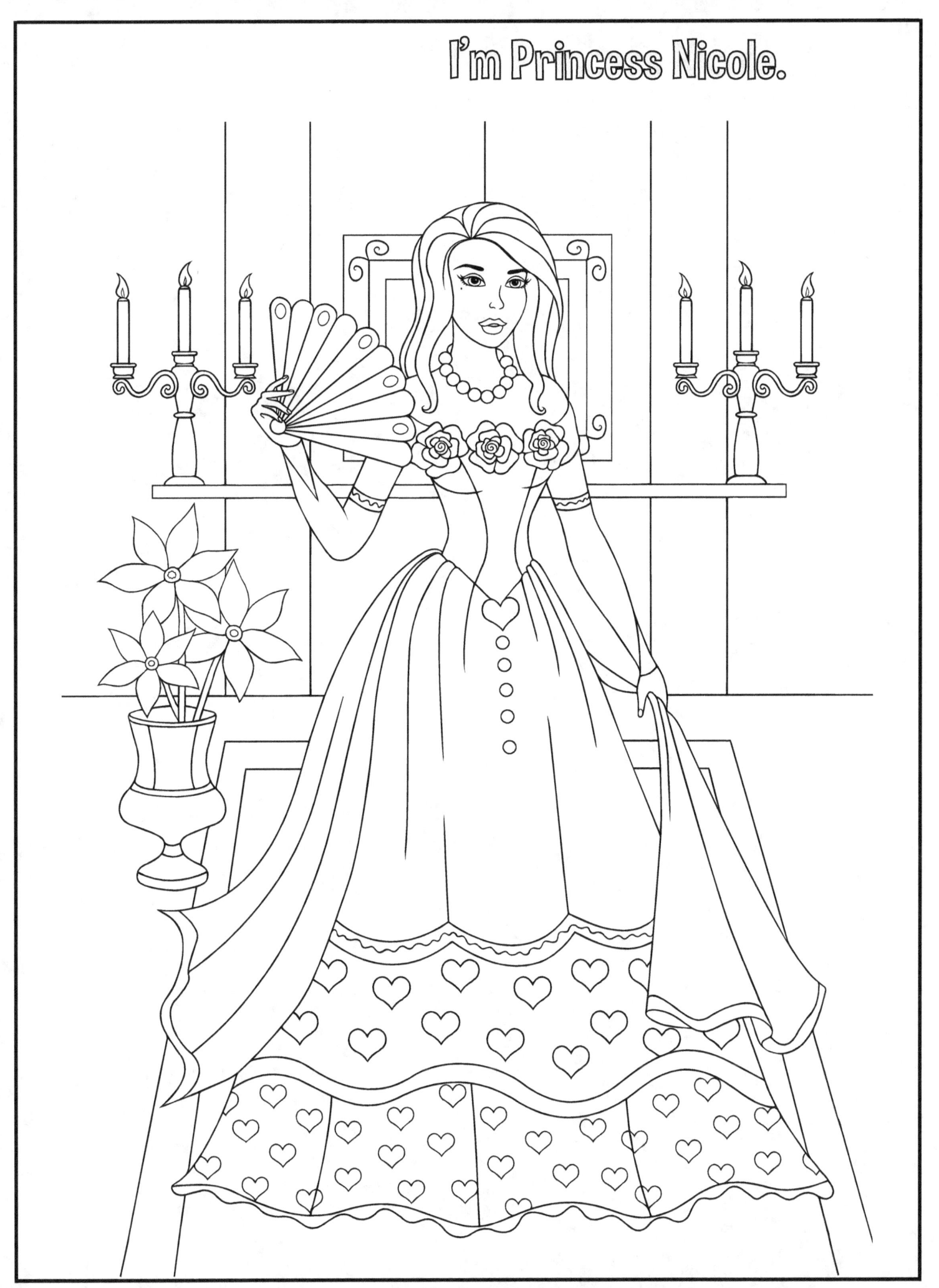

I'm Princess Nicole.

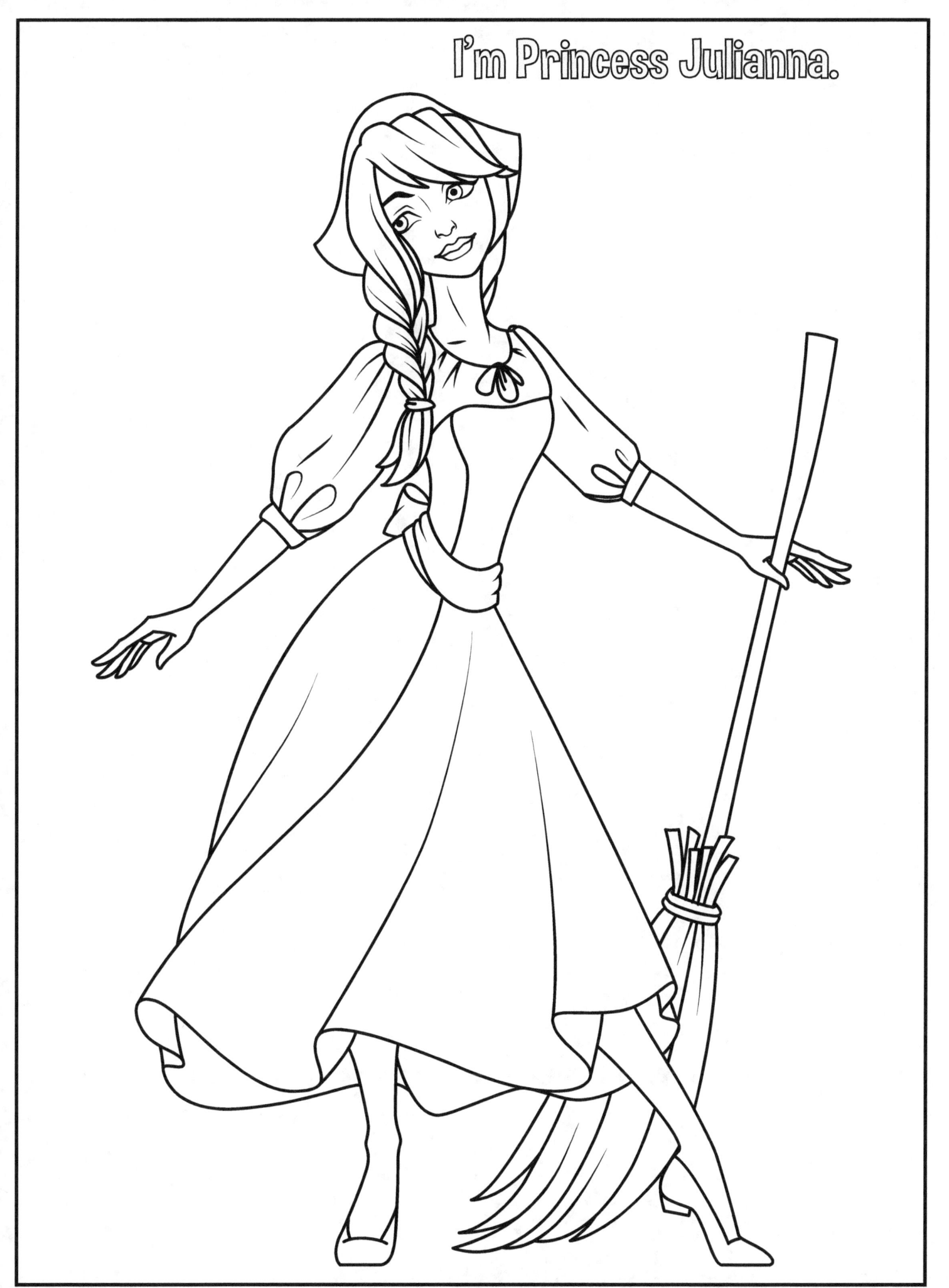

I'm Princess Julianna.

I'm Princess Olivia.

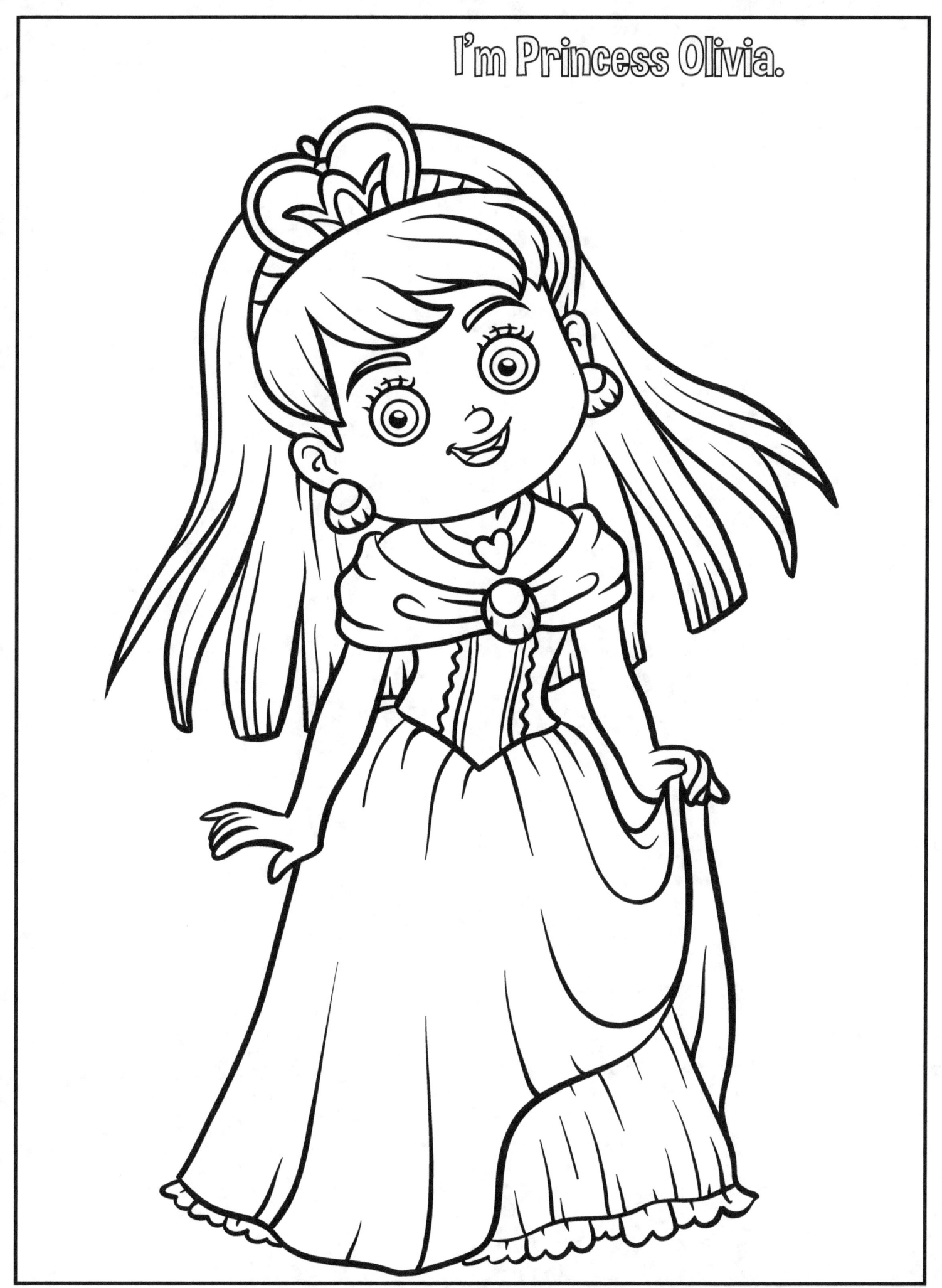

I'm Princess Emily.

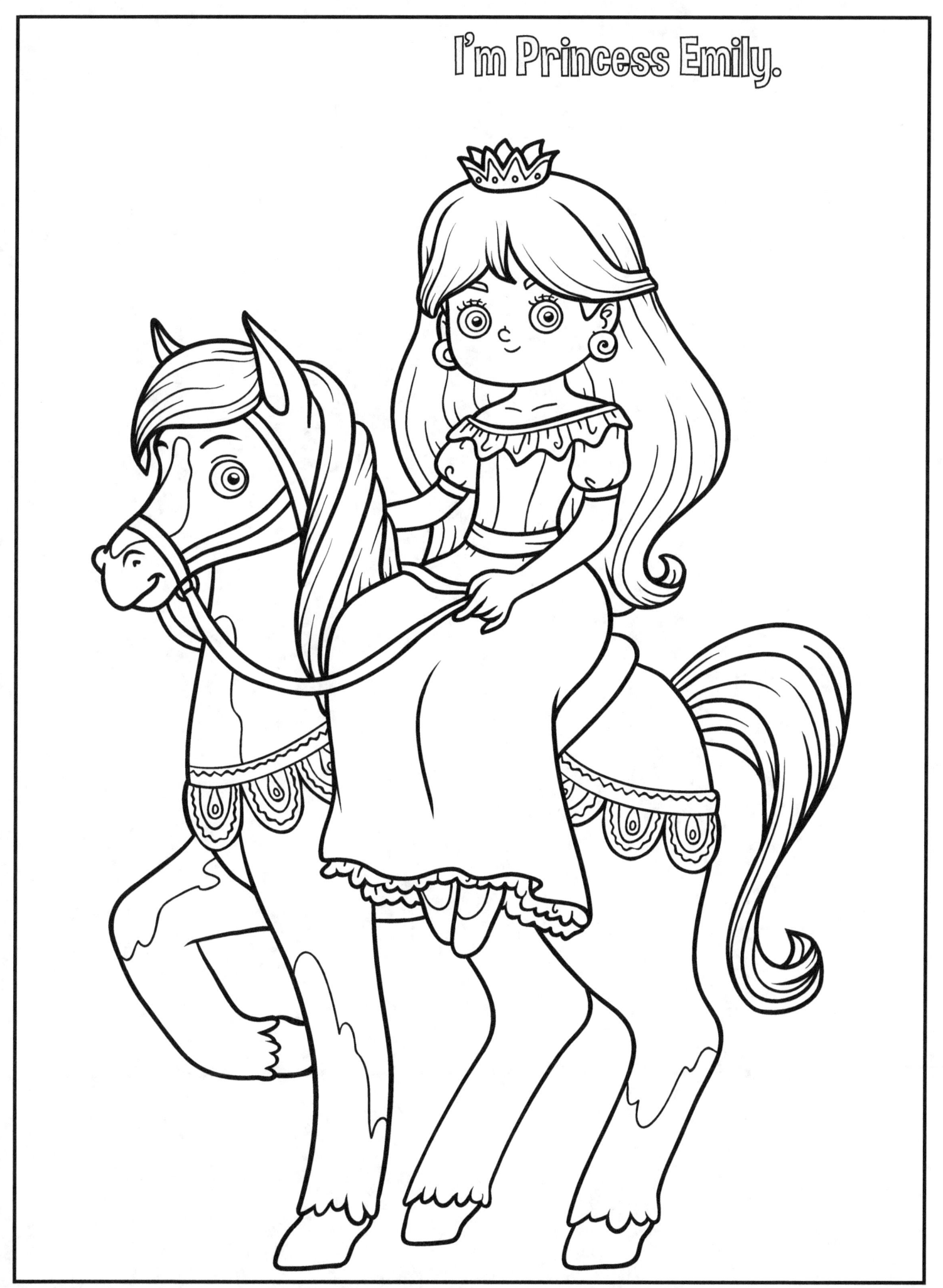

I'm Princess Caroline.

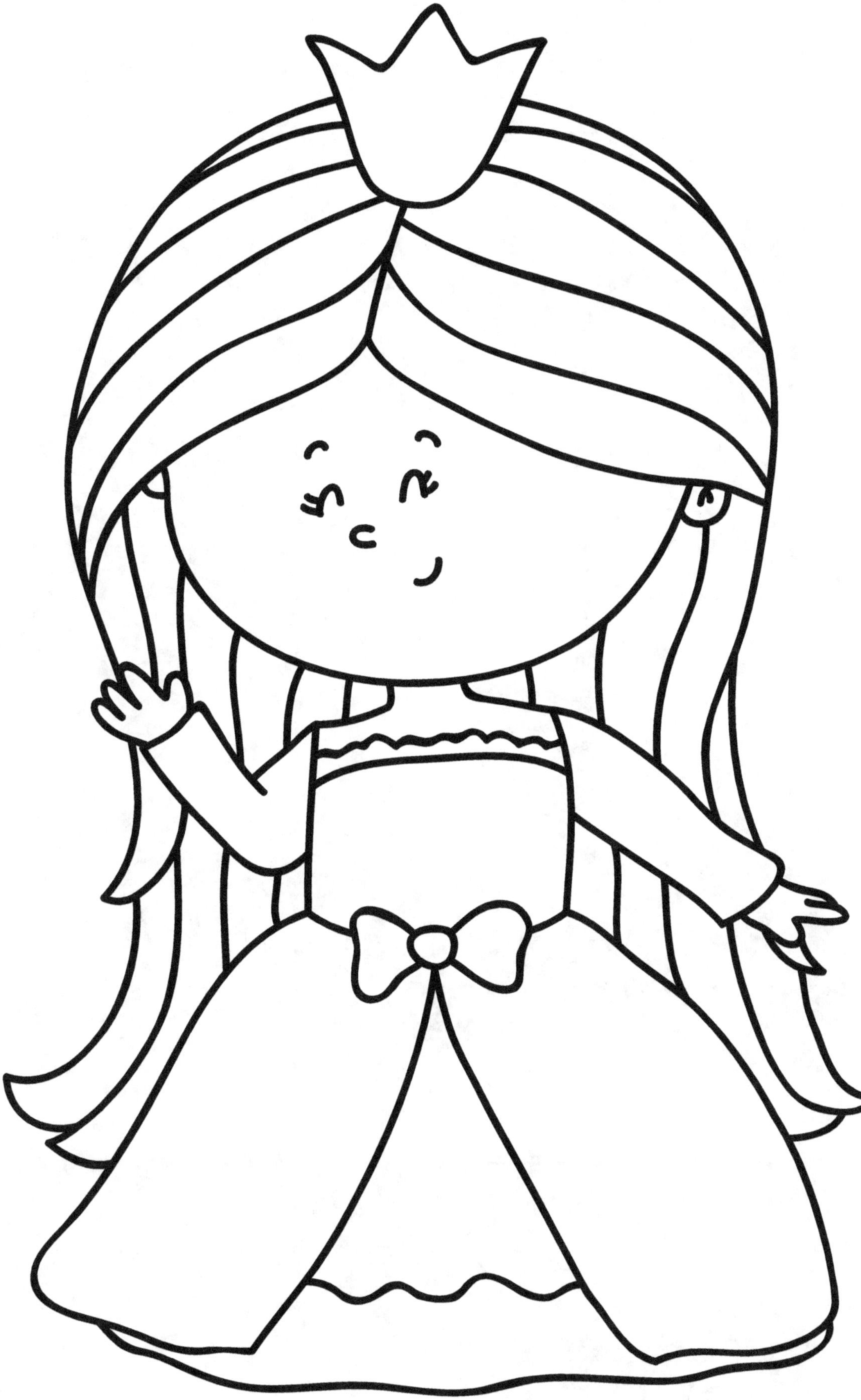

I'm Princess Lydia.

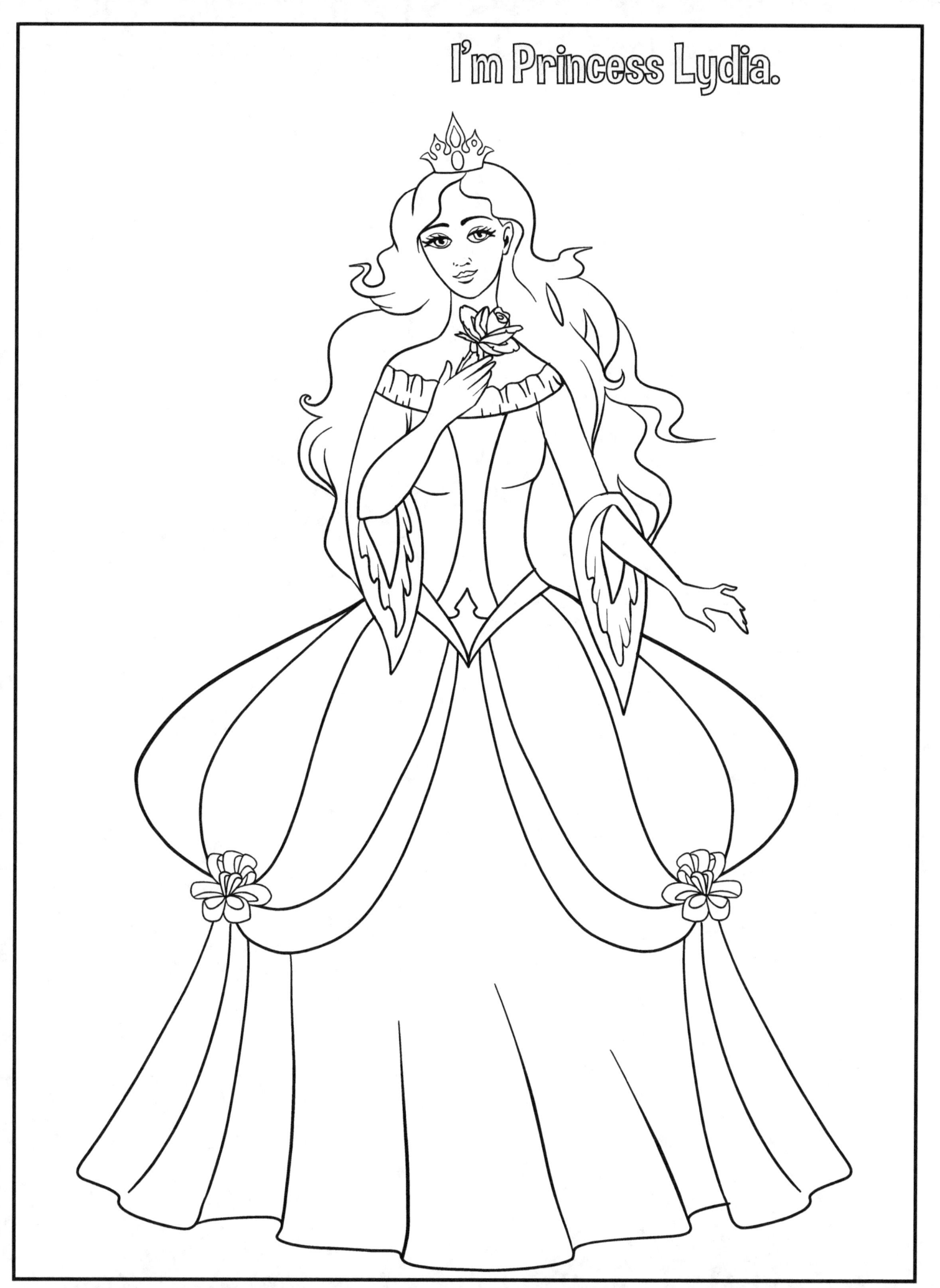

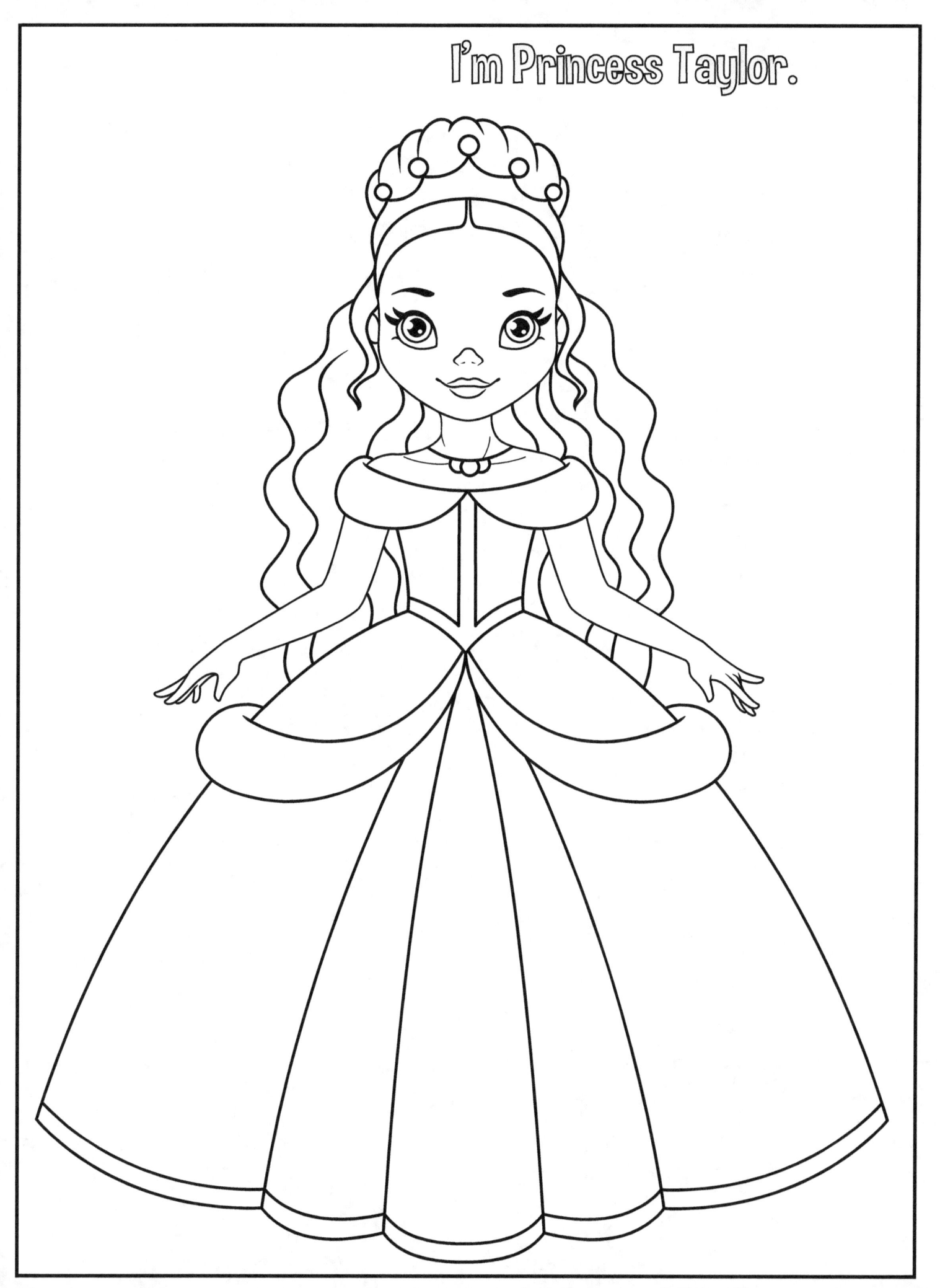

I'm Princess Taylor.

I'm Princess Eliza.

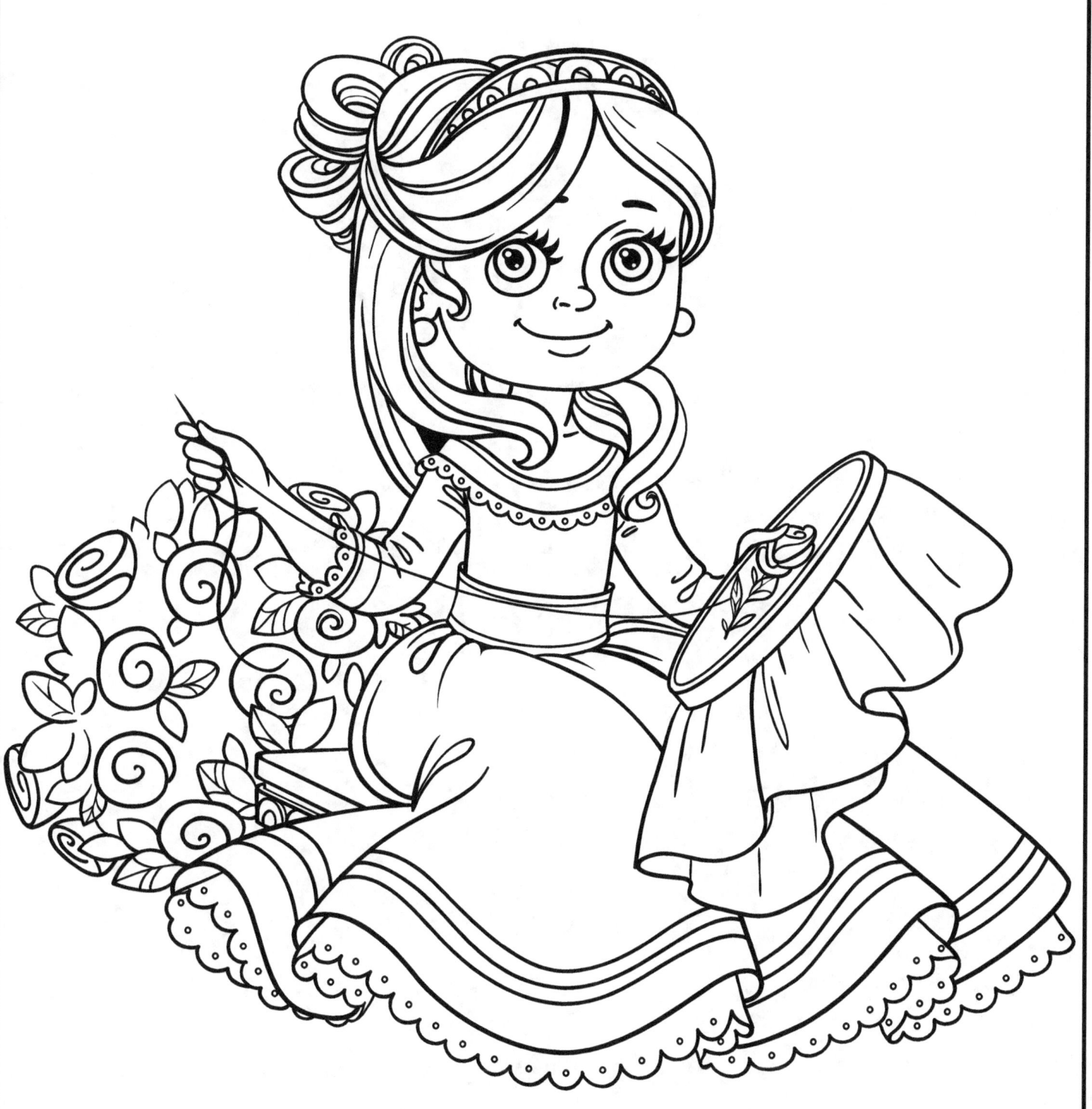

I'm Princess Daisy.

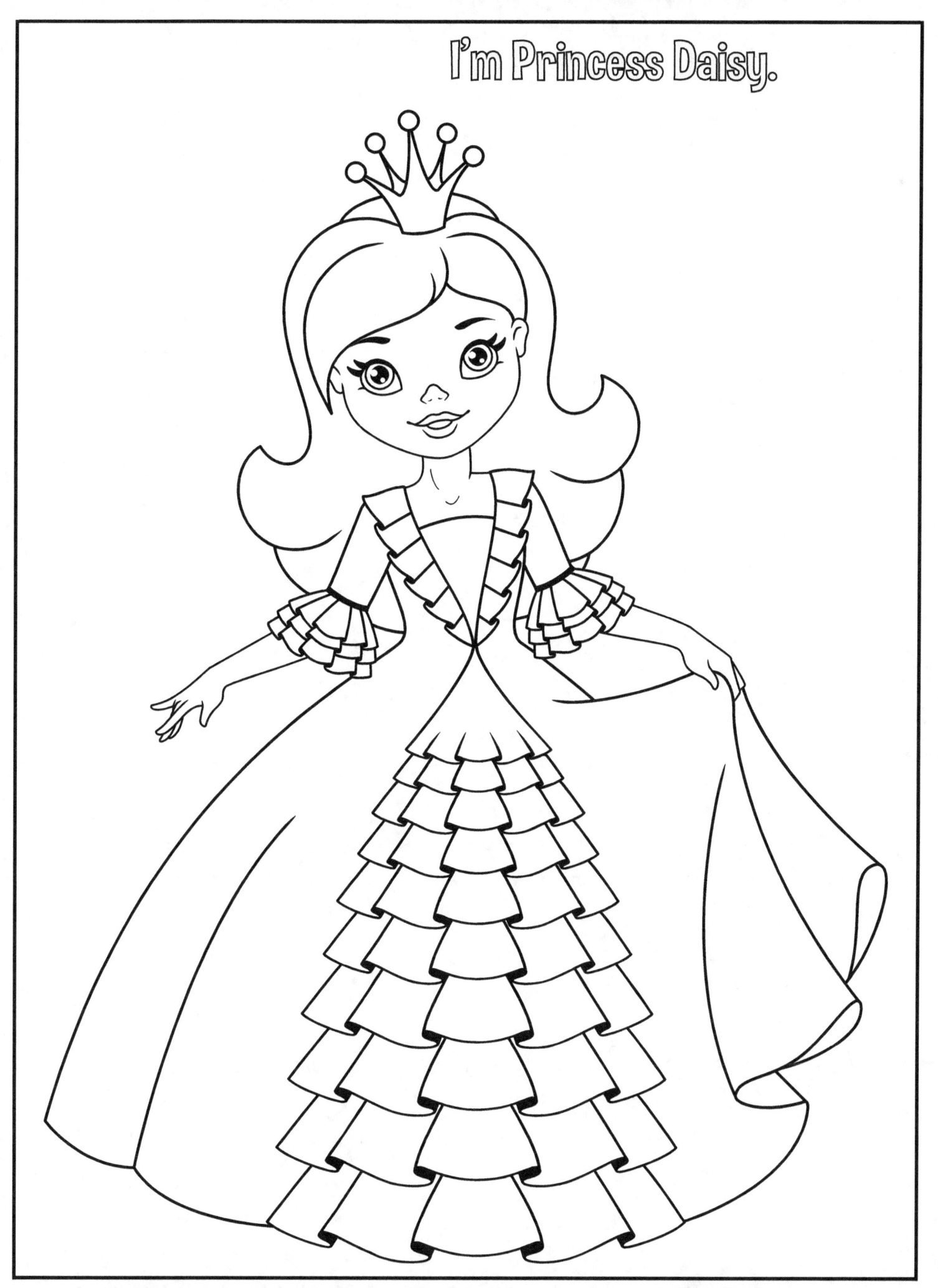

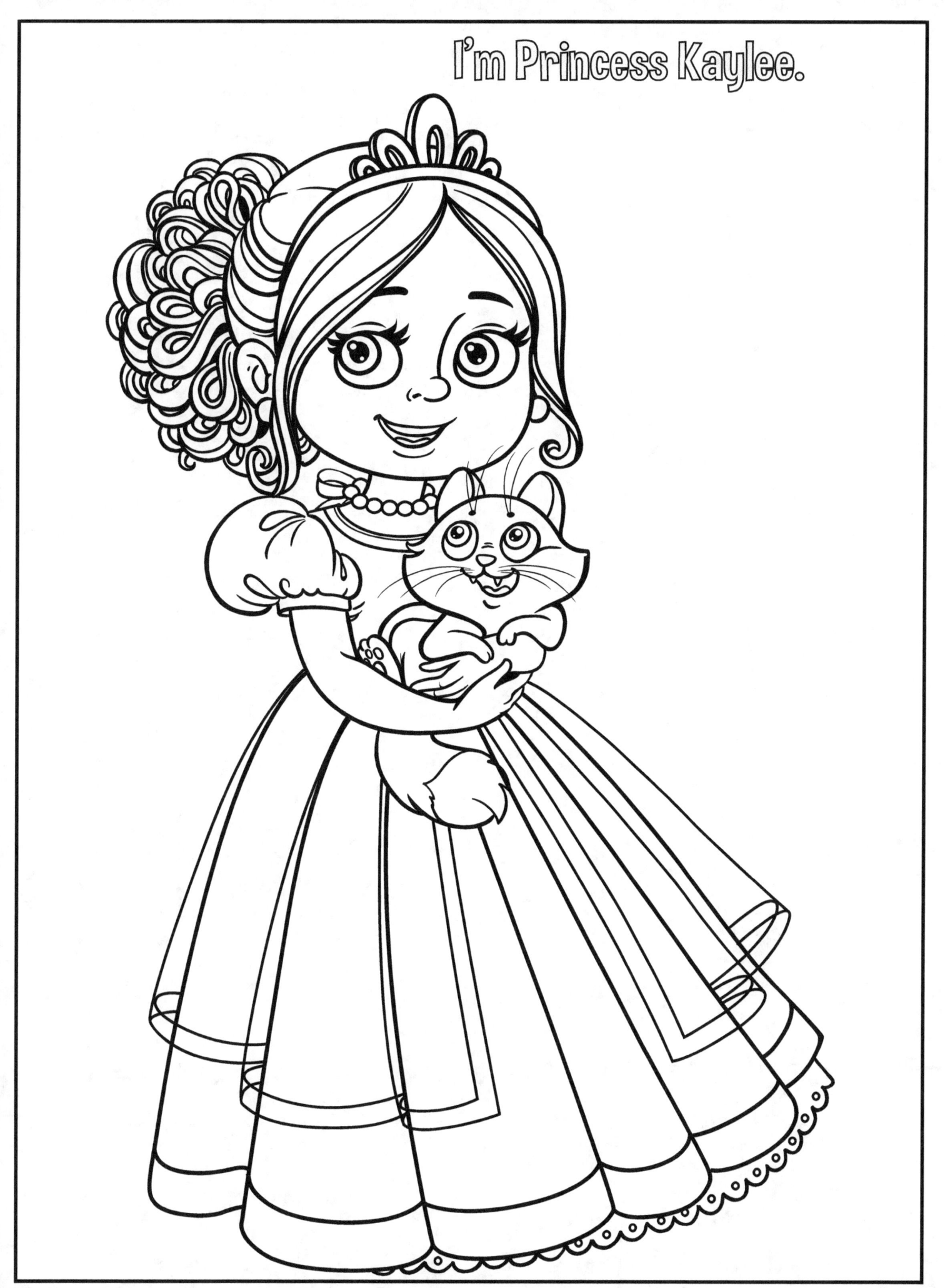

I'm Princess Kaylee.

I'm Princess Liliana.

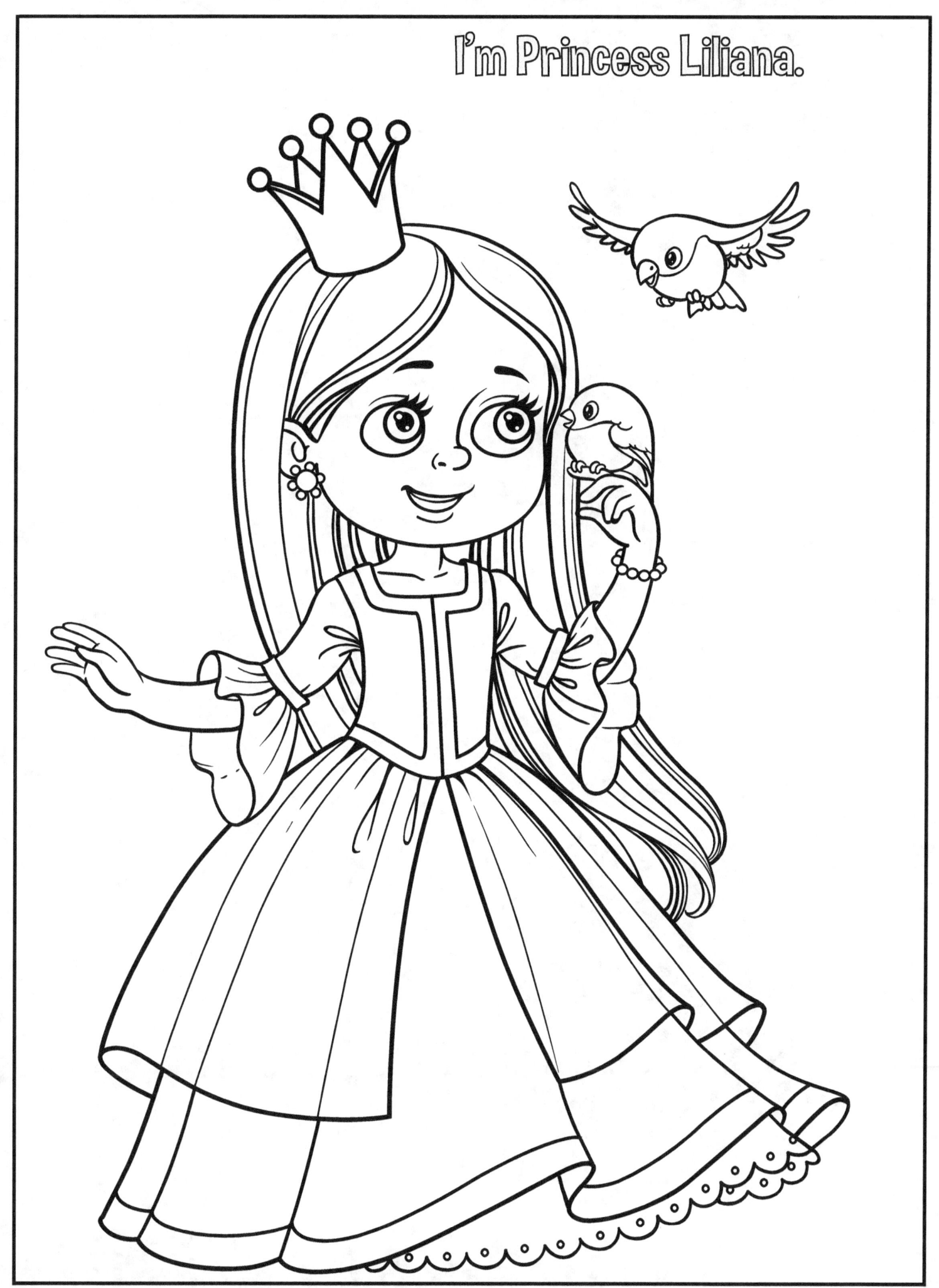

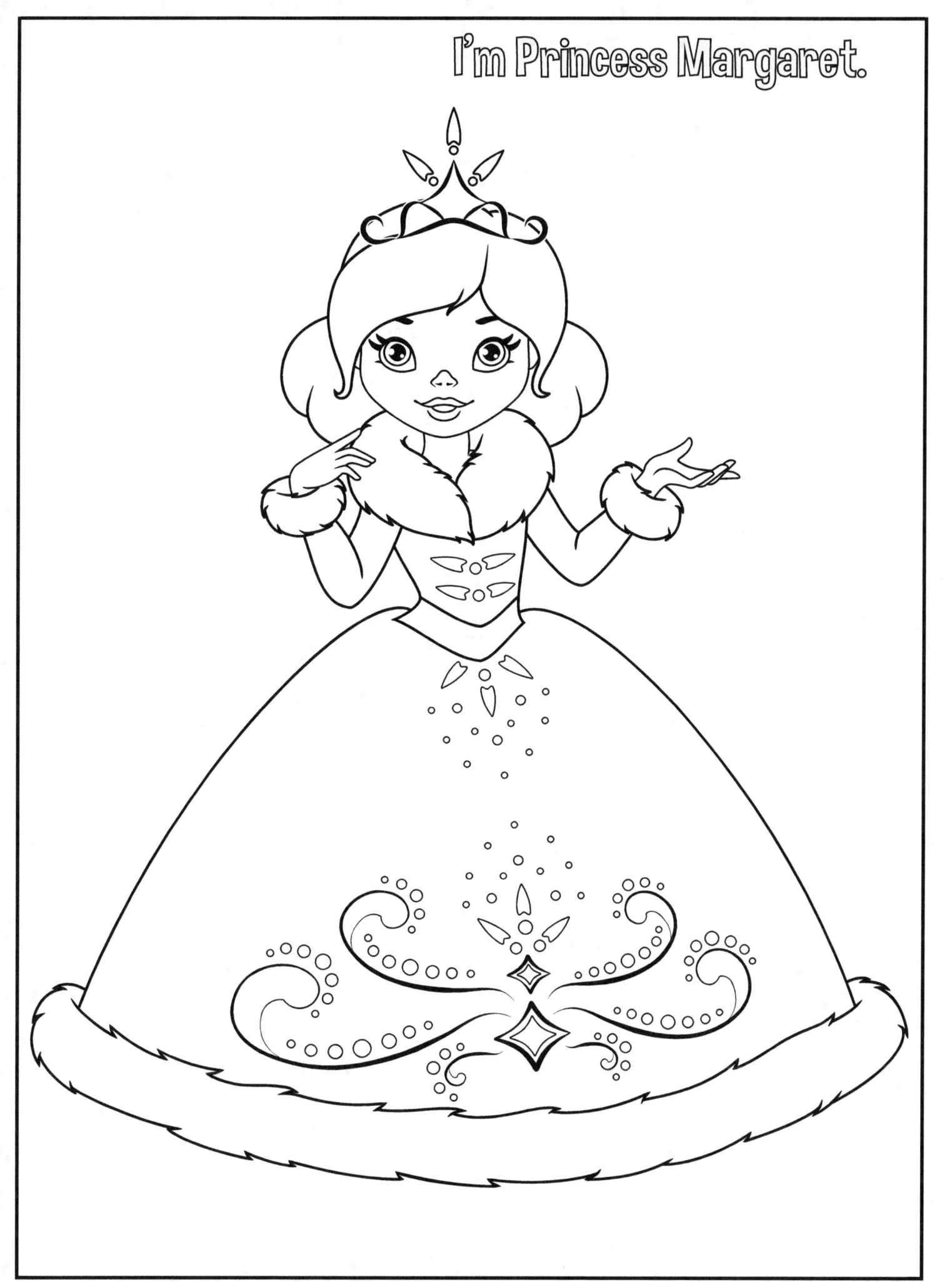

I'm Princess Margaret.

I'm Princess Rose.

I'm Princess Helen.

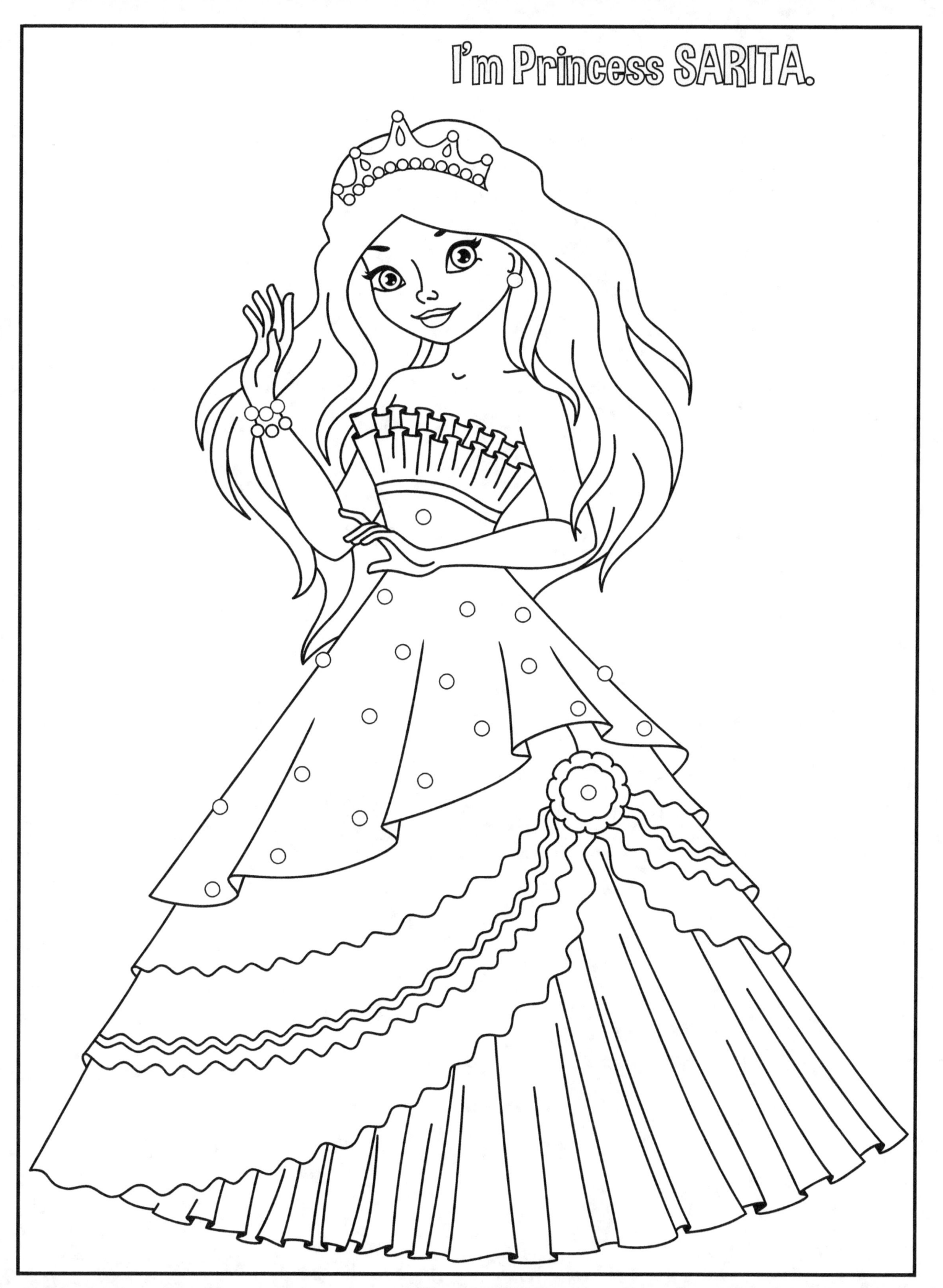

I'm Princess SARITA.

I'm Princess Alina.

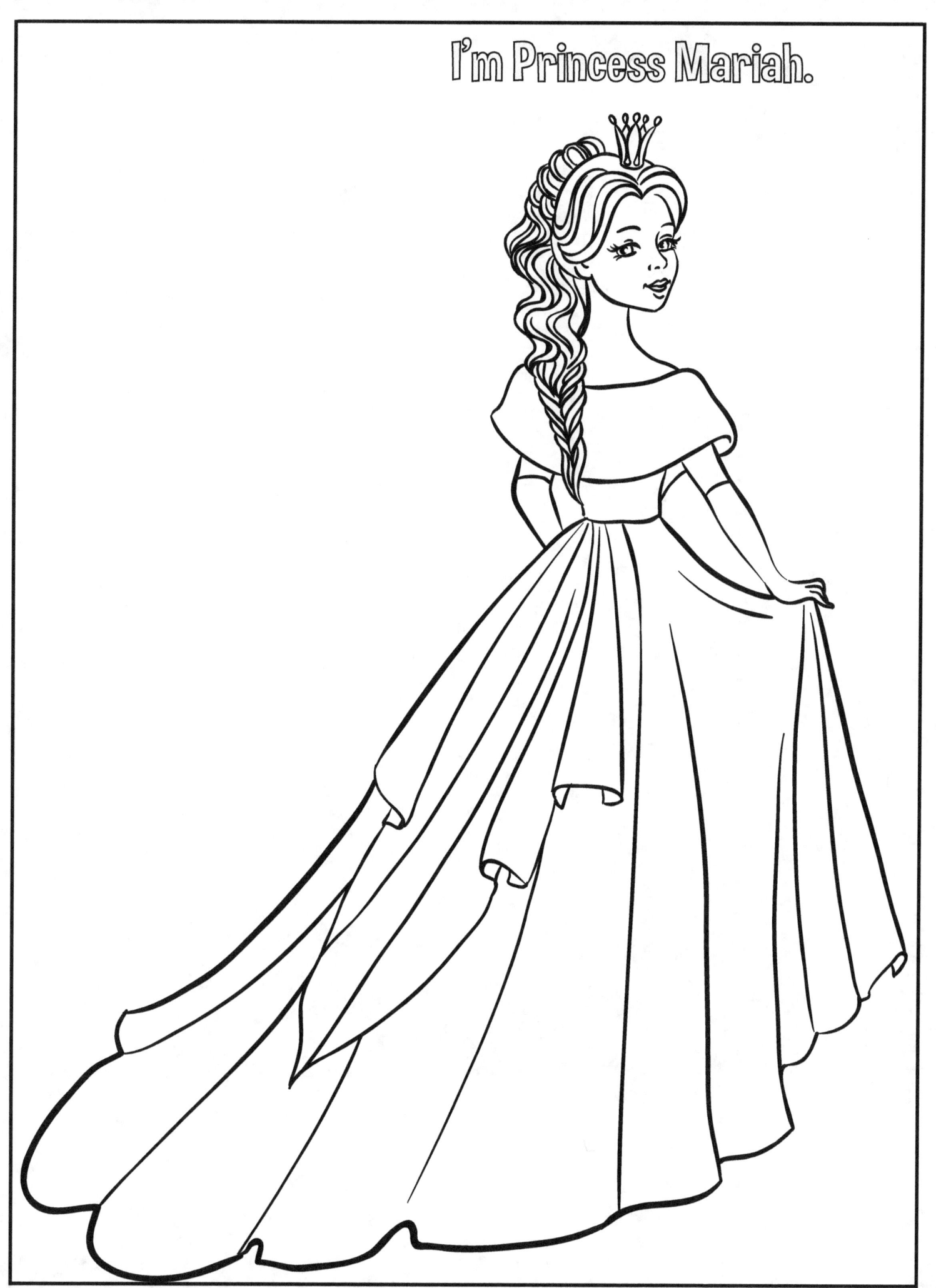

I'm Princess Mariah.

I'm Princess Rachel.

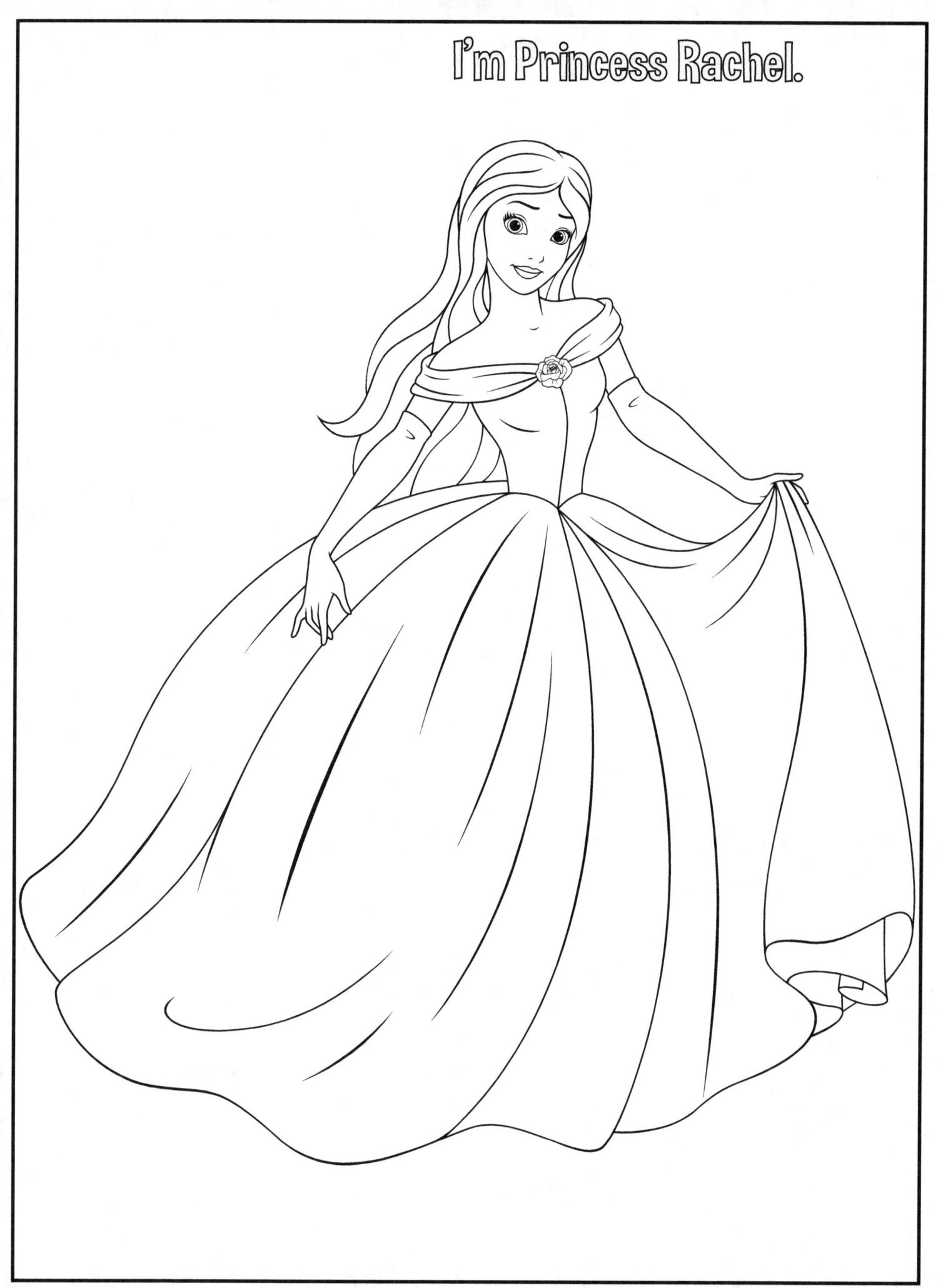

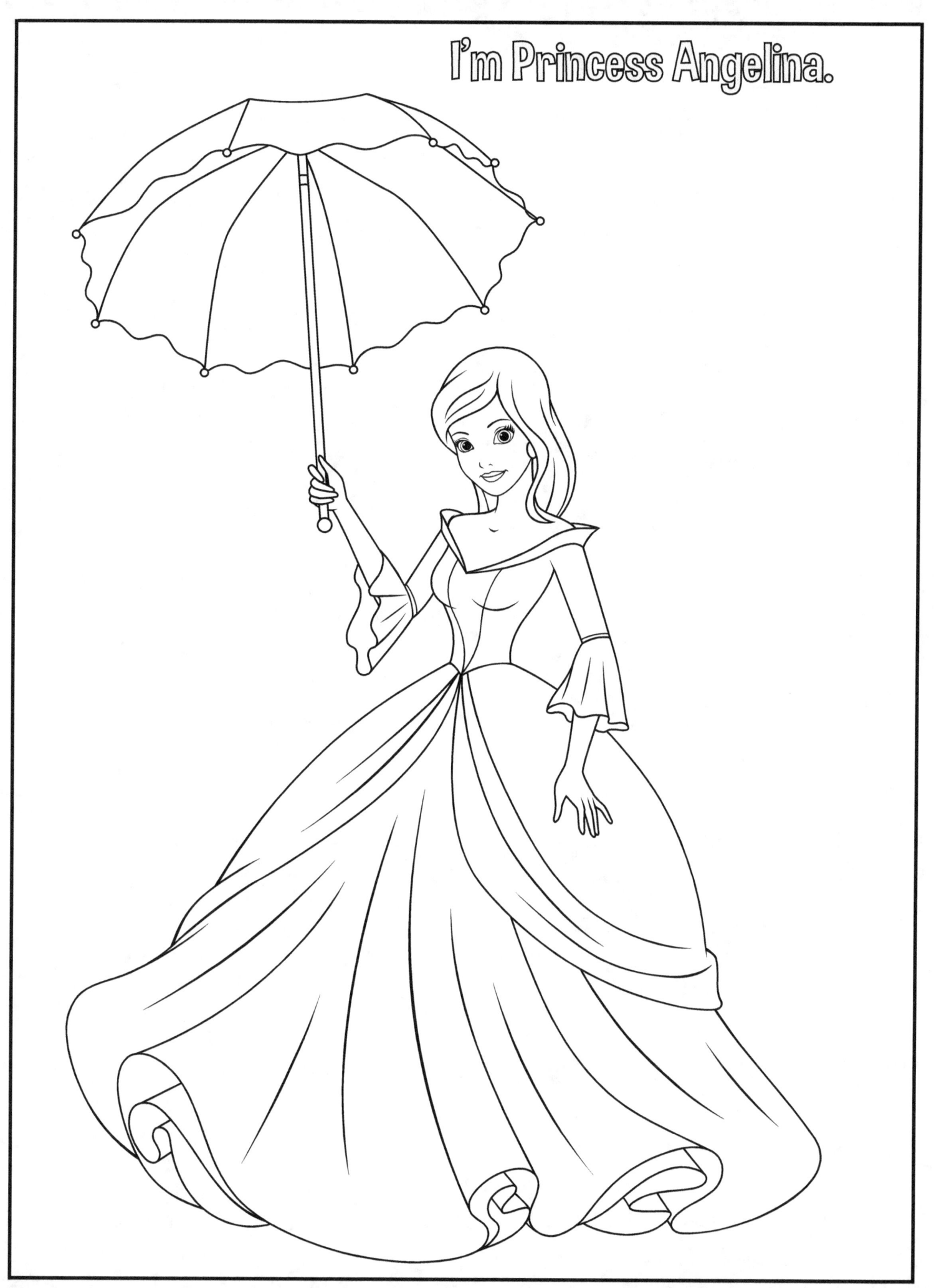

I'm Princess Angelina.

I'm Princess Harmony.

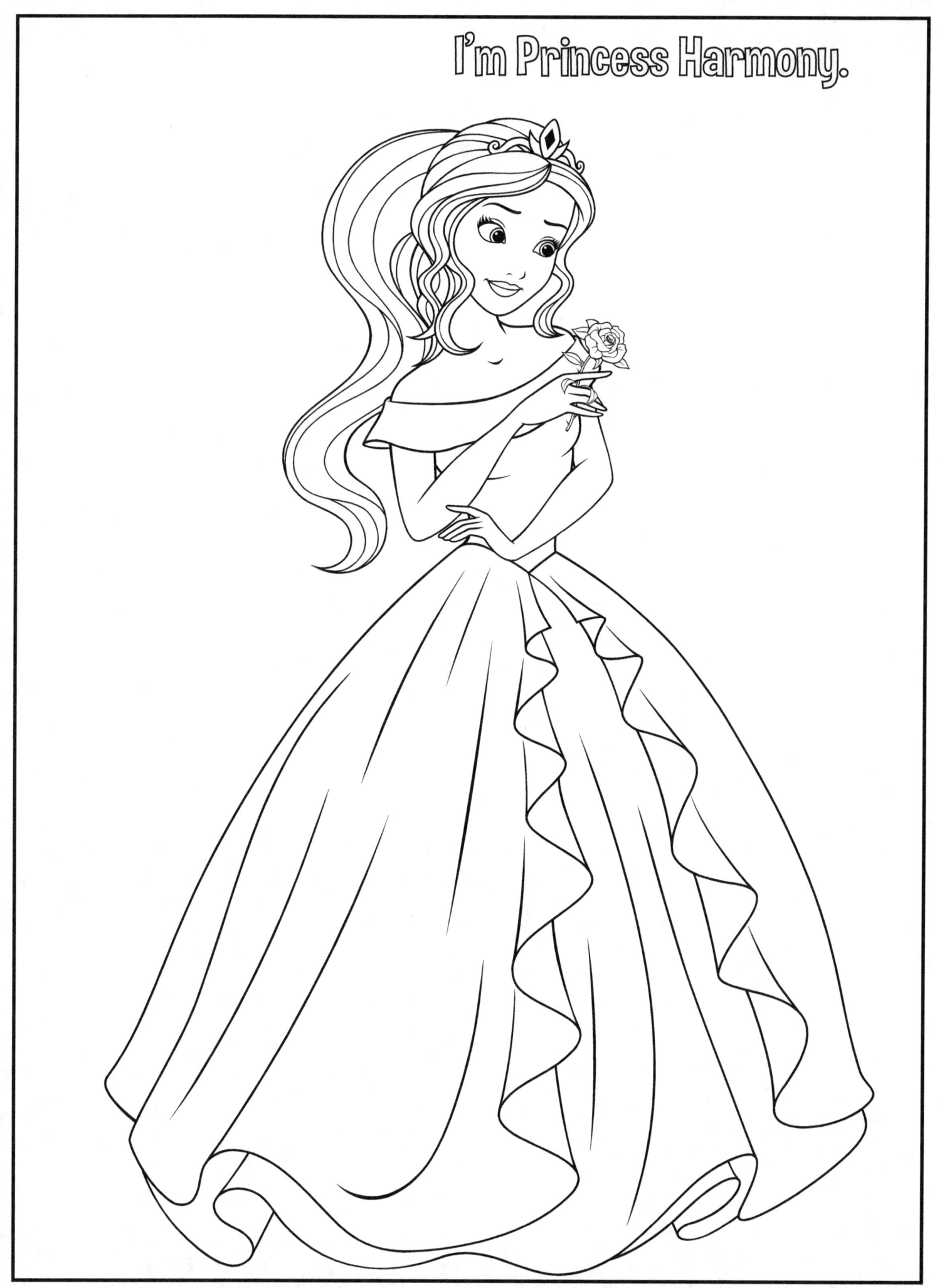

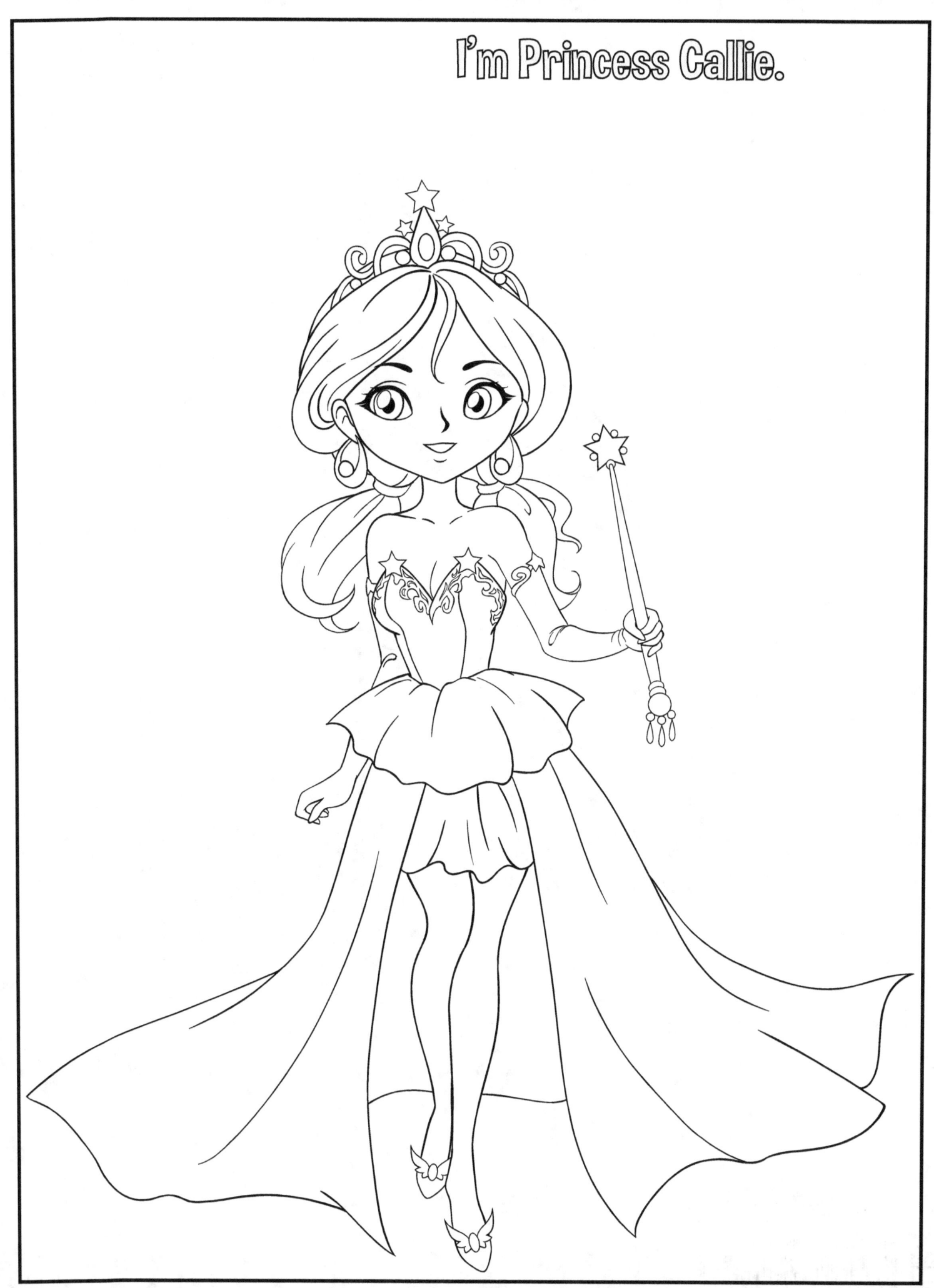

I'm Princess Callie.